Patient-Centric Analytics in Health Care

Patient-Centric Analytics in Health Care

Driving Value in Clinical Settings and Psychological Practice

James J. Gillespie and Gregory J. Privitera

LEXINGTON BOOKS
Lanham • Boulder • New York • London

Published by Lexington Books
An imprint of The Rowman & Littlefield Publishing Group, Inc.
4501 Forbes Boulevard, Suite 200, Lanham, Maryland 20706
www.rowman.com

Unit A, Whitacre Mews, 26-34 Stannary Street, London SE11 4AB

British Library Cataloguing in Publication Information Available

Library of Congress Cataloging-in-Publication Data Available

ISBN 978-1-4985-5097-0 (cloth : alk. paper)
ISBN 978-1-4985-5098-7 (electronic)

∞™ The paper used in this publication meets the minimum requirements of American National Standard for Information Sciences—Permanence of Paper for Printed Library Materials, ANSI/NISO Z39.48-1992.

Printed in the United States of America

We would like to dedicate this book to Stephanie Marie Dolliver, founder of Canvas for a CURE, a nonprofit charity with a mission to bring joy and courage to children who are diagnosed with cancer through canvas art and fundraising. Stephanie was intimately involved in the activities of her charity before taking a position at the Dana-Farber Cancer Institute. In all her work, Stephanie exemplifies a resilient style of leadership and selfless care for others that embodies the spirit of "patient centricity" that is at the heart of this book. Shortly after taking her new position, Stephanie herself was diagnosed with Hodgkin's lymphoma, a diagnosis that she is determined to beat.

Our thoughts and prayers are with you, Stephanie. May your embodiment of patient centricity that has inspired so many children bring you that same courage and resilience. You are a gift to anyone lucky enough to meet you, and you have so many more lives to touch! Stay #DolliverStrong.

For more information about Canvas for a CURE visit:
http://curekidscancer.com/canvas-for-a-cure/.

Contents

Acknowledgments

We would like to convey a special thank you to Rebecca Lawless, JD, for her invaluable copyediting and manuscript preparation support throughout the process of developing this book.

Introduction

The value of a health-care system is best measured by the quality, access, and costs associated with patient care. This perspective is at the core of what is meant by patient-centric analytics: the utilization of analytics to optimize quality, access, and cost measures connected to patient care. Enhanced quality of care, increased access to care, and lower costs to patients are vitally important considerations for the sustainability of any health-care system. While there is a wealth of data available across health care to inform decision makers, much of it is not fully utilized. Health-care sectors need to utilize these data, and analytics is the optimal tool to connect data to decision-making that drives value.

The health-care industry is under increased regulatory and financial pressures to deliver value, particularly as it relates to patient care in clinical and diagnostic settings. Analytics is a tool by which we can measure that value. Vast amounts of patient and organizational data are generated each day. At the patient level, analytics can be used to identify the most effective protocols for patient care, reveal best practices to minimize costs associated with care, and enhance detection of patients in greatest need of care, such as those who are at greatest risk of failing to follow a protocol (e.g., not taking their medications). Analytics can leverage the vast amounts of health-care data to drive value across the health-care ecosystem, from patient-centered medicine to provider-patient interactions and even preventive care (e.g., motivating patients to take charge of their health status).

Fundamentally, value for patients reflects value in the health-care system; if patients do not benefit in health care, then the system is not providing value to its key stakeholder. In this book, we introduce a new framework from which to navigate the vastness of the health-care system. The 6 Ps framework, illustrated in Figure 1.1 at the beginning of Chapter 1, identifies the 6 key inputs of the health-care system:

- patients
- policy makers
- providers
- pharmacies
- pharmaceuticals
- payers

The 6 Ps represent a comprehensive cross section of the health-care ecosystem with unique interests and motivations that drive decision-making. At the center of this framework are patients. A key perspective in this book highlights the use of analytics to improve communication across the 6 Ps with the goal of aligning their shared interests to enhance quality, increase access, and reduce costs connected to patient care. Driving sustainable, long-term value in a health-care ecosystem requires cooperative action across the 6 Ps, and analytics is a critical tool to accomplish this.

Outside of the health-care sector, there are an abundance of companies that optimize the use of data to inform or drive value for optimal customer experiences. Amazon, Google, and Facebook may be among the most widely known examples. Alternatively, within the health-care space, data and information can be segmented and hard to find. For example, retrieving the necessary information in an electronic health record (EHR), which is used to store and manage patient data, can be time-consuming and frustrating. EHRs contain vital patient information to guide clinical decision-making for the treatment and care of patients. Yet EHR data are often not shared in a standardized system, thereby creating a disconnect in patient data from one provider to another for the same individual.

There are many barriers to maximizing the use of analytics across the business (e.g., financial, operational) and clinical (i.e., the "front lines" of patient care) ends of the health-care system, although the tools needed to drive analytics in health care already exist in many forms. This book is structured to identify these barriers and to outline ways in which we can overcome them across the 6 Ps.

In Part I of this book, we introduce the 6 Ps framework (Chapter 1), the "fit" for analytics as a driver for decision-making across the 6 Ps (Chapter 2), many of the analytical tools available to drive value (Chapter 3), and key strategies for integrating and managing data for use in health care (Chapter 4).

In Part II, we evaluate the 6 Ps using a logical progression. With the focus on patient centricity, we naturally start at the center of the pentagonal framework with patients (Chapter 5), who elect the policy makers (Chapter 6), who then adopt the policies and guidelines for providers (Chapter 7), pharmacies (Chapter 8), and pharmaceuticals (Chapter 9) to follow. At the end of the process, those entities get reimbursed by the payers (Chapter 10).

In Part III, we evaluate best practices for leveraging analytics in health care. Best practices are evaluated for managing data quality to safeguard the systematic and meaningful use of data (Chapter 11), managing data queries and sampling from data banks and resources (Chapter 12), and utilizing data to drive actionable decisions and bridge the gap between data and information (Chapter 13). We close with an overview of the value created by analytics to make health care "smarter" (Chapter 14).

Throughout this book, we evaluate the role of the 6 Ps from a patient-centric analytics approach. A key focus is on value for patients, which reflects value in the health-care system itself. Using a 6 Ps pentagonal framework, we hope this book can expand your understanding of the vastness of the health-care system and the extent to which data can be leveraged using analytics to optimize decision-making that can ultimately benefit the key stakeholders in the system: the patients.

Part I

THE LANDSCAPE OF DATA ANALYTICS

Chapter 1

A Pentagonal Framework for the 6 Ps in Health Care

A CONCEPTUAL FRAMEWORK

Strictly defined, analytics is the systematic analysis of data or statistics to obtain information that has value and can be utilized. There is a wealth of data in health-care organizations (HCOs), but much of it is never transformed into useful information. In today's climate, HCOs are under increased regulatory and financial pressures to deliver *measurable* value, particularly as it relates to the quality of patient care in clinical and diagnostic settings. Data that can promote value in HCOs is just waiting to be analyzed in ways that have not yet been addressed. This is where the need to *utilize* data becomes apparent—where analytics comes into focus for health care.

Vast amounts of patient and HCO data are generated each day. Whether we are concerned about patient-centered medicine, barriers to health care, behavioral health, provider-patient interactions, or preventive care, in all cases we can utilize data that HCOs accumulate every day to deliver *measurable* value.

This idea of *measurable* value is particularly important. A health-care firm or a counseling clinic, for example, may claim to provide value to a community. The question is how to measure that value, which is the importance, usefulness, or worth generated by *deliverables* in a given system. The deliverables are the tangible (e.g., cure disease) or intangible (e.g., provide peace of mind for patients) outputs produced by the inputs of a health-care system or entity.

Throughout this book, we will identify the health-care space using a 6 Ps framework, as illustrated in Figure 1.1. The 6 Ps are key inputs in the health-care system that have the largest impact on value. One P, however, stands out when identifying value: patients. Health care is an industry created to serve

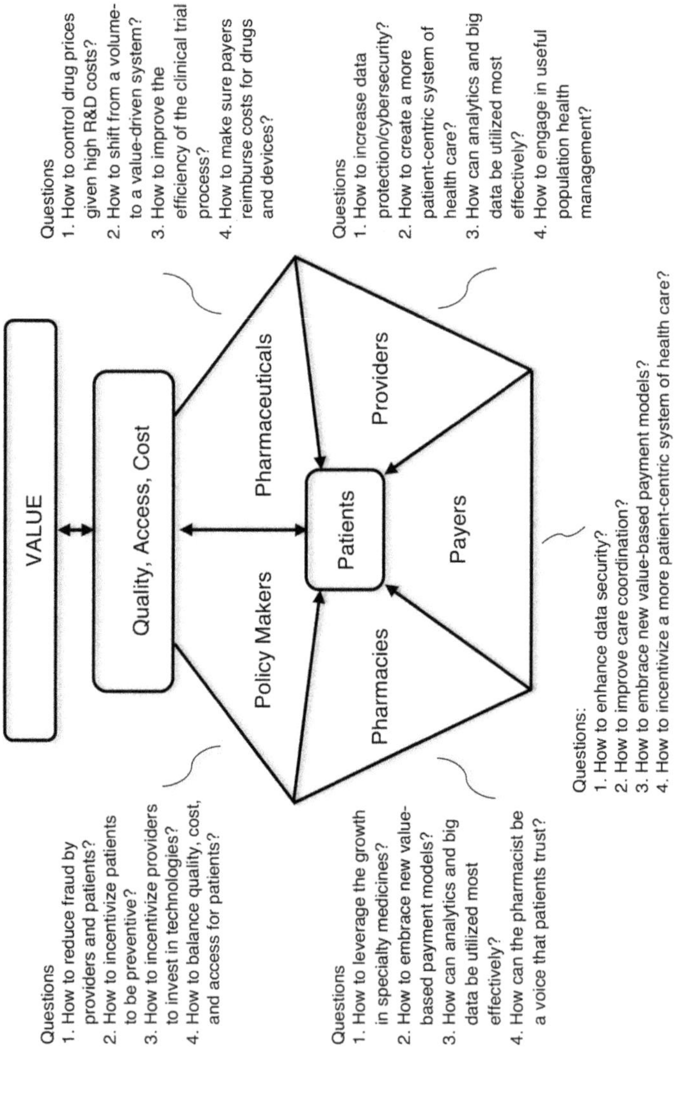

Figure 1.1 A Pentagonal Framework for the Landscape of Analytics in Health Care.

the needs of patients, which places them at the center of any analytics model for health. This is the perspective from which we write this book.

Notice in Figure 1.1 that *value* is the key output for health care. Fundamentally, value for patients reflects value in the health-care system; if patients do not benefit in health care, then HCOs are not providing value to their key stakeholders. That said, the inputs of the system (i.e., the 6 Ps) largely impact our ability to drive value in health care and in clinical settings. Ultimately, we can measure the "effect" of these inputs in terms of three broadly defined variables identified in Figure 1.1:

- Quality—the standard or degree of excellence of care; measured across the industry from systems (e.g., the utility of diagnostic procedures) to patients directly (e.g., the effectiveness of an implemented treatment plan)
- Access—ease at which patients can utilize care in the system; the system is most effective when all patients can utilize the system for care
- Cost—expenditures required to make the system efficient in terms of time, money, and resources

Throughout this book we identify value in health care as a function of quality, access, and cost, which is driven largely by the 6 Ps. Understanding the role of the 6 Ps and the utility of analytics to promote data-driven decision models can lead to new innovations that can drive *value* in the health-care system.

The 6 Ps identified in Figure 1.1 and throughout this book are as follows:

- patients
- policy makers
- providers
- pharmacies
- pharmaceuticals
- payers

In Part II, we evaluate the 6 Ps starting at the center of the pentagonal framework with patients (Chapter 5), who elect the policy makers (Chapter 6), who then adopt the policies/guidelines for providers (Chapter 7), pharmacies (Chapter 8), and pharmaceuticals (Chapter 9) to follow. At the end of the process, those entities get reimbursed by the payers (Chapter 10). Throughout Part II we evaluate the role of the 6 Ps from a *patient-centric analytics* approach using the pentagonal framework that was illustrated to open this book. In this chapter, let us first take a brief look at each of the 6 Ps, which play such a vital role in driving value in health care.

PATIENTS

Patients are at the center of any model for health care. Ultimately, HCOs exist to serve the needs of patients. While it may be most expensive to care for sick patients, it is also true that many industries in health care actually serve healthy patients. Many industries aim to keep patients healthy, not necessarily treat them just when they are sick. Consider the following phrases patients can often say:

- "Let's just relax and go to bed early; it has been a stressful day."
- "I eat more organic foods to stay healthy."
- "Spending time with my dog cheers me up."
- "I feel energized when I exercise; it makes me feel better."
- "I am going to physical therapy every day to improve my recovery."

These statements all relate to the concerns of patients, yet only the last statement relates to illness. It should be clear that health is not relevant only when patients are ill. Therefore, HCOs serve the needs of patients across the illness-wellness continuum from health and wellness to sickness and recovery. Across this continuum, patients often have the benefit of industries that directly partner with them, such as patient advocacy groups and patient-driven services like WebMD.

As technologies and medicine advance, patients increasingly have a greater stake in their own health. There is a culture shift in health care from a *physician-centered communication model* (communication is directed from physician to patient) to a more collaborative *patient-centered communication model* where the patient is part of the team of caregivers.[1] Indeed, in spirit of communication, the National Patient Safety Foundation (NPSF) started the "Ask Me 3" program to improve communication between patients and health-care providers.[2] This program encourages patients to be active, collaborative members of their health-care team, and to ask the following three questions to enhance patient-provider communications:

- What is my main problem?
- What do I need to do?
- Why is it important for me to do this?

1 Privitera, G. J. (2016). Health Psychology. In C. McCarthy, M. DeLisi, A. Getzfeld, G. J. Privitera, C. Spence, J. Walker, . . . C. Youssef-Morgan (Eds.), *Introduction to Applied Behavioral Science* (pp. 32–54). San Diego, CA: Bridgepoint Education.

2 National Patient Safety Foundation / Institute for Healthcare Improvement. (2017). *Ask Me 3*. Retrieved from http://www.npsf.org/?page=askme3.

These questions, of course, presume an encounter with a physician regarding illness. Yet the concerns of patients extend beyond illness. Encompassing the full scope of patient needs can drive increased value in health care. Analytics can be a key tool for identifying ways to increase value for patients by looking beyond "Ask Me 3" to a broader set of questions that patients often ask:

- How to be more preventive?
- How to be a researcher regarding one's own health?
- How to leverage technology to increase convenience and transparency?
- How to be a full member of one's own health-care team given the era of patient centricity?
- How to take on the role of a money manager given increasingly high deductibles and coinsurance?

There are growing databases of patient information stored in EHR systems, and analytics is key to utilizing these data in meaningful ways, specifically to increase value. There is a real interest in analyses that lead to recommendations for personalized care. For patients, this encompasses *quality* (e.g., at a patient-provider level), *costs* (e.g., out-of-pocket), and *access* (e.g., patient portal, mobile patient access records, care), which in turn drive *value* in health care. We specifically examine the role of patients for driving value in health care in Chapter 5.

POLICY MAKERS

Policy makers are those institutions or groups who have the ability to directly influence governmental policies that can affect the inner workings of the health-care system. Policy makers set the stage for value in health care via their instrumental role in establishing a culture of care for patients and for key stakeholders in the system.

The types of institutions, associations, and groups that constitute policy makers in health care can be found at all levels of government and in private industry. Policy makers include the following:

- Federal government (e.g., the US Department of Health and Human Services (HHS) and the National Institutes of Health)
- state, county, and local governments
- nongovernmental organizations (NGOs) and think tanks (e.g., the American Enterprise Institute and the Brookings Institution)
- professional associations (e.g., the American Psychological Association and the American Medical Association)
- industry and trade groups (e.g., the American Hospital Association)

Policy makers influence policy directly or indirectly related to patient care. They ask important questions that often evaluate macro-level needs in the health-care system. Many types of questions asked across policy-maker industries are given in Figure 1.1, and a few additional questions are added here, all of which can be evaluated using analytical tools:

- How to reduce fraud and abuse by providers?
- How to incentivize patients to be preventive?
- How to incentivize providers to invest in technology?
- How to balance quality, cost, and access for patients?
- How to create a more patient-centric system of health care?
- How to be more collaborative across industry and organizational boundaries?
- How to encourage the continued movement from a volume-based system to a value- and risk-based system?
- How to incentivize providers and payers to leverage analytics and big data most effectively?

Policies that impact health care can, in turn, impact *quality* of care, *access* to care, and *costs* of care as part of "doing business." Thus, policy makers can have a direct and an indirect impact on the efficiencies of creating value in the health-care system. We specifically examine the role of policy makers for driving value in health care in Chapter 6.

PROVIDERS

Providers are the hospital systems, centers, clinics, individual practices, and agencies that provide care directly to patients. Providers are at the front lines of delivering value in the health-care system by interacting with patients, both directly (e.g., delivering a treatment) and indirectly (e.g., making health information more accessible to patients via flyers and pamphlets).

The types of hospital systems, centers, clinics, individual practices, and agencies that constitute providers in health care can be found at all levels of government and in for-profit and not-for-profit systems. Some examples are as follows:

- Federal government (e.g., Veterans Affairs hospital systems)
- state, county, and local governments (e.g., public clinics and health agencies)
- hospitals
- integrated delivery networks
- medical centers
- physician group practices

- community clinics
- retail clinics
- urgent clinics
- nursing homes and other long-term care facilities
- allied health practices (e.g., acupuncture, chiropractic, dentistry, homeopathy, and massage therapy)

Providers ask important questions that evaluate or impact patient care. Many types of questions asked across provider industries are given in Figure 1.1, and a few additional questions are added here, all of which can be evaluated using analytical tools:

- How to increase data protection and cybersecurity?
- How to create a more patient-centric system of health care?
- How can analytics and big data be utilized most effectively?
- How to engage in effective population health management?
- How to be more collaborative across industry and organizational boundaries?
- How to continue doing Medicare and Medicaid in a fiscally responsible manner?
- How to become better at telehealth, home health care, and community-based care?
- How can technological advancements be leveraged to enhance quality, improve efficiency, reduce costs, and grow revenue?

Providers play a large role to deliver *quality* of patient care. By and large, providers would embrace efficiencies to reduce costs associated with health care, while increasing *access* and *quality* of care to patients. We specifically examine the role of providers for driving value in health care in Chapter 7.

PHARMACIES

Pharmacies are the industries where medicinal drugs are dispensed and sold. They make medications, prescriptions, and health devices accessible to patients. Pharmacies enhance the *access* patients have to health resources they need in a way that is increasingly convenient. The growing number of options includes the following:

- pharmacy chains (e.g., CVS Health, Rite-Aid, Walgreens Boots Alliance)
- local pharmacies
- online pharmacies
- pharmacy benefit managers (e.g., Catamaran and Express Scripts)

Pharmacy industries ask important questions that largely impact the access that patients have to medications, prescriptions, and health devices. Many types of questions asked across pharmacy industries are given in Figure 1.1, and a few additional questions are added here, all of which can be evaluated using analytical tools:

- How to leverage the growth in specialty medicines?
- How to embrace new value-based payment models?
- How can analytics and big data be utilized most effectively?
- How can the pharmacist continue to be a voice that patients trust?
- How to continue integrating clinical services and retail operations?
- How to be more collaborative across industry and organizational boundaries?
- How can the pharmacist develop a more robust role as a key member of the health-care provider team?

Pharmacies deliver *access* to care, largely in terms of dispensing medicinal drugs. While other Ps, such as policy makers, tend to play a bigger role in driving up or down *costs* associated with medicines and health devices, pharmacies can enhance *quality* (of medicine prescription) and *access* (to medicine). We specifically examine the role of pharmacies for driving value in health care in Chapter 8.

PHARMACEUTICALS

Pharmaceuticals represent a diverse cross section of industries in medicine and the life sciences that primarily create the following products: large molecule drugs (i.e., biotechnologies), small molecule drugs (i.e., pharmaceuticals), and medical devices (e.g., heart valve, X-ray machine, tongue depressor, hospital bed, stethoscope, etc.). Organizations and companies that make pharmaceuticals used in medicine and health care fall into this category. The pharmaceuticals and products that are produced often are cutting edge and represent innovation on a scale that is unique to health-care markets.

Large global life science companies like Merck and Pfizer tend to have both biotechnology and pharmaceuticals. These innovations are usually used to fight diseases (e.g., various cancers), but some are used for preventive medicine or for diagnosis. The medical device industry is usually separate from the biopharma industry, although the two merge for items like a prefilled syringe, which is both a device and a drug. Medical devices can be preventive, diagnostic, or curative.

The types of organizations and companies that constitute pharmaceuticals in health care can be found across the health and life science disciplines. Pharmaceutical industries include the following:

- biotechnology companies (e.g., Amgen, Biogen, Celgene Corporation, Gilead Sciences, and Regeneron Pharmaceuticals)
- medical device companies (e.g., Johnson & Johnson, General Electric, Siemens, Medtronic, and Baxter)
- pharmaceutical product-producing companies (e.g., Merck, Novartis, Pfizer, Roche, and Sanofi)
- pharmaceutical wholesalers (e.g., AmerisourceBergen and McKesson)
- contract research organizations (e.g., Quintiles, Covance, PAREXEL, ICON, and inVentiv Health)

Organizations and companies that innovate pharmaceuticals and products ask important questions that evaluate what care is available, how care is delivered to patients, and what advances in care are possible. Many types of questions asked across these industries are given in Figure 1.1, and a few additional questions are added here, all of which can be evaluated using analytical tools:

- How to control drug prices given high R&D costs?
- How to shift from a volume- to a value-driven system?
- How to improve the efficiency of the clinical trial process?
- How to make sure payers reimburse costs for drugs and devices?
- How to be more collaborative across industry and organizational boundaries?
- How to integrate new products such as biosimilars and personalized medicine?

It can be quite expensive to develop pharmaceuticals and products, which makes *costs* associated with these industries vitally important. On the whole, these industries would embrace efficiencies to reduce costs while increasing *quality* of care and *access* patients have to care. We specifically examine the role of pharmaceuticals for driving value in health care in Chapter 9.

PAYERS

Payers are the organizations and businesses that provide insurance and payment to offset health-care expenses for patients. Payers have a high stake in the *costs* of health care and a vested interest in driving costs down in health-care markets.

The types of organizations and businesses that constitute payers in health care allow many patients to participate in a health-care system that would otherwise be too expensive for them to afford. Payers include the following:

- government (e.g., Centers for Medicare & Medicaid Services (CMS))
- private insurers (e.g., Aetna, Anthem, Blue Cross Blue Shield Association, UnitedHealth Group)
- self-insured employers (e.g., Boeing and Intel)

Payer industries ask important questions that largely impact costs of care and efficiencies in providing care. Many types of questions asked across payer industries are given in Figure 1.1, and a few additional questions are added here, all of which can be evaluated using analytical tools:

- How to enhance data security?
- How to enhance care coordination?
- How to embrace new value-based payment models?
- How to create a more patient-centric system of health care?
- How can analytics and big data be utilized most effectively?
- How to engage in effective population health management?
- How to incentivize preventive care by patients and providers?
- How to operate in an era of increased patient fiscal responsibility?
- How to be more collaborative across industry and organizational boundaries?
- How to accommodate increased consumer demand for transparency (e.g., cost comparison tools, price estimates, billing clarity)?

Payers play an important role in health care by being in a unique place in the market. Since payers pay for many of the costs in the system, they have a vested interest in driving down those costs. We specifically examine the role of payers for driving value in health care in Chapter 10.

HCOs and the Need to Think Outside the Box

HCOs face real challenges in that they are highly resistant to change. Indeed, many industries have embraced analytics. Amazon, Google, and Facebook, for example, readily apply analytical tools to create an engaging, tailored, user-friendly experience for customers and website visitors—experiences that are largely driven by algorithms and data that specifically utilize customer search histories and preferences.

The tools needed to drive analytics in health care therefore already exist in many forms. Yet in health care, the use of analytics is relatively dearth. While search engines have streamlined the process for obtaining information available online, no comparable tools exist for efficiently sorting through the tremendous quantities of data stored within HCOs. For example, accessing EHRs, which are used to store patient data, can be quite challenging. Retrieving the necessary information that you are searching for in an EHR can be time-consuming and frustrating. This and other barriers to the effective utilization of analytics in health care are discussed at greater length in the chapters to follow.

Given that analytics is widely used outside of health care, in each chapter of this book we include a feature called "Thinking Outside the Box." These are testimonials from leading experts across industries where analytics have been employed successfully. By sharing real-world experiences, each expert provides insights as to how analytics can be effectively utilized. In the feature for this chapter, we evaluate the "bigger picture" of analytics.

THINKING OUTSIDE THE BOX: FINDING *VALUE* WITH ANALYTICS

Laurie Branch, President, Iroquois® Group

To figure out how much to charge you for your auto insurance, some insurance companies have started using telematics. This allows insurers to offer usage-based insurance rates that take into account your driving behavior. What is telematics? It is a telecommunications device you install in your vehicle that allows the insurance company to monitor exactly how you drive. It can tell the company if you brake hard frequently, take a turn at too high of a speed, or tend to accelerate rapidly. It can also tell when you are driving and even where you drive by using GPS data. Normal insurance policies take into account your age, gender, driving record, the miles you typically drive, and where you are likely to drive based on information you provide on the insurance application. This information allows them to use statistics to "guess" at your driving habits and come up with a rate for your policy. But with telematics, they can observe your driving habits and get a much better idea of the likelihood that you will be in an accident. This allows them to enhance *value* for their customers by offering preferential rates to people who use their cars less and who drive conservatively.

Applying Analytics in Health Care

At a macro-level, analytics can be applied in three different approaches to address the diverse set of questions asked in this chapter:

- Descriptive analytics visualizes and explores data using graphing, modeling, and some inferential statistics. This analytics approach uses techniques

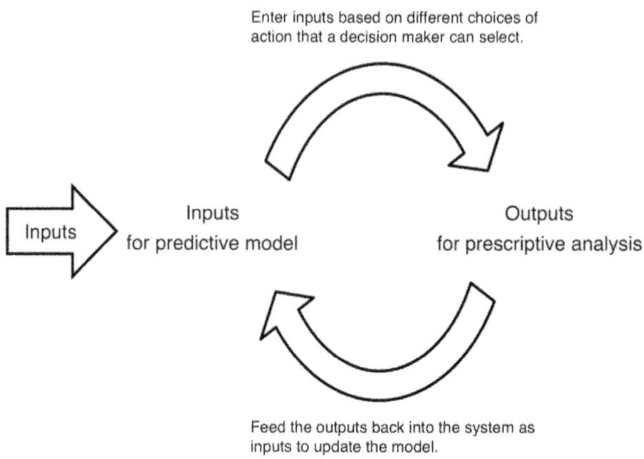

Figure 1.2 The General Structure of Prescriptive Analytics.

such as data aggregation, data modeling, and probability functions to provide insights into the meaning of the data we have access to. Descriptive analytics answers, "What has happened?"

- Predictive analytics are statistical analyses used to predict outcomes by examining existing data for patterns or relationships to make inferences forward in time. This analytics approach identifies relationships that exist between data elements or variables to predict or forecast future outcomes to inform decision-making. In a way, we basically take data that we have to predict data that we do not have using inferential statistical models, simulations, and forecasting techniques. Predictive analytics answers, "What could happen?"
- Prescriptive analytics includes descriptive and predictive analytics to find or "prescribe" the best course of action for a given situation. Using a prescriptive model, described in Figure 1.2, we (a) enter existing data as inputs to a predictive model to produce outputs that inform different choices of action, and then (b) feed the outputs back into the system as inputs to update the model based on possible consequences for the different choices of action that a decision maker can select. This analytical approach uses optimization and algorithms to advise decision makers on possible outcomes. Prescriptive analytics answers, "What should we do?"

Each analytical approach has the ability to help HCOs demonstrate value in health care via data-driven decision models that extrapolate meaningful use of data. Therefore, throughout this book we refer to each of these analytical approaches to identify the potential value of analytics for health care. As you read, we encourage you to consider how the 6 Ps drive *quality*, *access*, and *cost*—the key measures of the *value* that a health-care system provides. By applying, throughout this book, the unique pentagonal framework identified in Figure 1.1, we hope you will see how the 6 Ps can impact health care, and how HCOs can employ analytical approaches to effectively utilize the vast amounts of resources and data available.

REFERENCES

National Patient Safety Foundation / Institute for Healthcare Improvement. (2017). *Ask Me 3.* Retrieved from http://www.npsf.org/?page=askme3.

Privitera, G. J. (2016). Health Psychology. In C. McCarthy, M. DeLisi, A. Getzfeld, G. J. Privitera, C. Spence, J. Walker, . . . C. Youssef-Morgan (Eds.), *Introduction to Applied Behavioral Science* (pp. 32–54). San Diego, CA: Bridgepoint Education.

Chapter 2

Taxonomy of Analytics in the Health-Care Space

BUILDING FROM A PENTAGONAL FRAMEWORK

A key challenge across the spectrum of health care is to not only deliver but also *measure* deliverables in a way that can show *value*. Recall that *value* is the importance, usefulness, or worth generated by deliverables in a given system, and a *deliverable* is a tangible (e.g., cure disease) or intangible (e.g., provide peace of mind for patients) output produced by the inputs of a given system or entity. The 6 Ps are key inputs in the health-care system. While the interests of the 6 Ps can be quite diverse, there is also substantial overlap built largely by the common interest that they share: To deliver value to patients.

Across the 6 Ps there is a broad range of concerns that ultimately impact quality, access, and cost. Analytics can be applied across this spectrum, which encompasses outcomes that are business related (e.g., costs, profitability, operations) and outcomes that are clinically related (e.g., disease, diagnosis, patient safety). Figure 2.1 illustrates this taxonomy for the health-care space, which we call the "healthscape."

The taxonomy identified in Figure 2.1 is not comprehensive, but it does address a key perspective for analytics: The potential for analytics in health care is vast. HCOs record tremendous amounts of data every day. Whether the questions being asked are on the business end or on the clinical end, analytics can be effectively used to supply answers.

Notice also in Figure 2.1 that the business and clinical components of health care can overlap. Fraud and data security, for example, can fall on the clinical or business end of the spectrum, depending on the specific issues being addressed. Clinical concerns can include securing patient data to ensure privacy to patients, or developing protocols to ensure proper identification of patients (e.g., proper surgical procedures). Business concerns can include

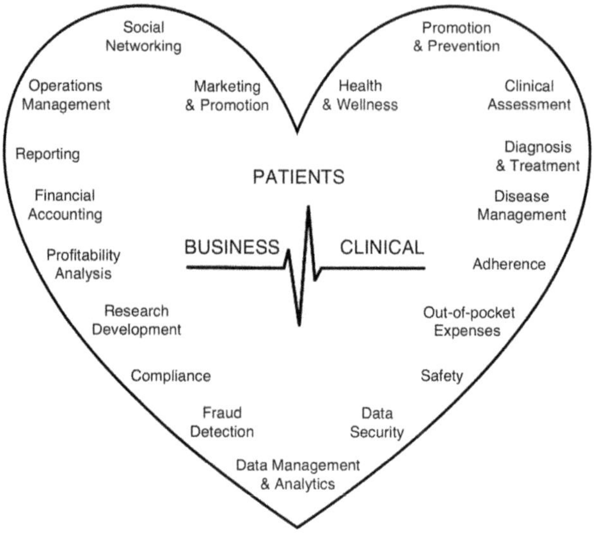

Figure 2.1 The "Heart" of the Healthscape: A General Taxonomy.

identifying fraud detection procedures to reduce fraud and the costs associated with it, or developing compliance protocols to enhance organizational efficiencies.

Ultimately, the "heart" of the healthscape taxonomy captures the diversity of interests and questions that can be asked in health care. Health care in business and clinical settings has diverse interests, yet also interests that overlap. Applying analytical tools to address these questions can provide a systematic framework that can tap into a variety of diverse needs and interests that are unique to health-care industries. It may seem overwhelming that analytics can have such a wide-ranging utility in health care, but it can and it has across many other industries. In the "Thinking Outside the Box" feature for this chapter, we look at how basic analytics are being utilized in franchise industries to promote business needs while balancing those of the customers they serve.

THINKING OUTSIDE THE BOX: CONSUMER SERVICE AS A KEY FACTOR TO ACHIEVING *VALUE*

Andrew J. Privitera, Franchise Owner, Chick-fil-A, Omaha, NE

At Chick-fil-A, analytics are utilized in all aspects of our business to guide decision-making and bring *value* to customers. The average

Chick-fil-A restaurant generates over $4 million dollars in annual revenue, serving nearly 2,000 guests a day. Service is a main factor to achieving value at Chick-fil-A, with a key challenge being how to consistently serve fresh food, accurately and fast. Our success in serving customers is guided largely by utilizing analytical tools. For example, iPads are posted at food-prep stations throughout the kitchen and show average sales for each 15-minute period of the day, thereby allowing us to prep the correct amount of food (fresh). Hundreds of reports are generated to show our sales mix (accuracy), customer profiles (great service), labor analytics (speed), and more. Chick-fil-A is the No. 1 growing quick-service chain in the United States. As a franchise owner, I can confidently affirm that analytics is a key tool utilized to achieve this success.

Evaluating the Healthscape Taxonomy Across the 6 Ps

Across the 6 Ps, the healthscape is dynamic. Change is truly a constant in health care. The types of questions and the nature of the questions being asked must be adaptive to the evolving delivery and nature of health care. By extension, the analytical tools that health-care professionals use to answer those questions must be equally adaptive to change. In Chapter 3, we will begin to take a closer look at the diverse set of analytical tools available to health-care professionals. However, in this chapter, let us first revisit the types of questions that each of the 6 Ps asks across the spectrum of the healthscape taxonomy, from business to clinical.

PATIENTS

Health care, as an industry, is becoming increasingly patient-centric. What this means is that increasingly the value that the 6 Ps provide is measured by how effectively they serve the needs of patients. Whether technologies advance medicines or clinicians identify more sensitive diagnostic tests, the goal is to serve the needs of patients who are the "customers" in the health-care system.

In Chapter 1, we shared many of the core types of questions that patients ask. As one would expect, for patients, the questions tend to focus largely on the clinical end of the healthscape taxonomy. Clinically related questions can pertain to health and wellness,

- How to be more preventive?
- How to be a researcher regarding one's own health?

or clinical assessment,

- How to be a full member of one's own health-care team given the era of patient centricity?

or out-of-pocket expenses and adherence,

- How to leverage technology to increase convenience and transparency?
- How to take on the role of a money manager given increasingly high deductibles and coinsurance?

While cost is a key concern for patients as it relates to their access to care, the questions they ask largely focus on the clinical end of the healthscape taxonomy. Of all the 6 Ps, patients have the highest "stakes" in health care because, for them, the outcomes could be life or death, such as in cases of terminal illness. Having *access* to *quality* affordable health care is a fundamental concern for patients.

POLICY MAKERS

Health-care policy is about adapting to change—identifying policies that, if implemented, could enhance the *quality* of care, *access* to care, and *costs* of "doing business" to promote a stronger patient-centric ideal. For policy makers in health care, it is therefore vital to understand the role of policy in achieving what is commonly referred to as the "Triple Aim":[1]

- better care for individuals (including quality and satisfaction)
- better care for populations
- lower health-care cost trends per capita

In Chapter 1, we shared many of the core types of questions that policy makers ask, each of which is directly or indirectly related to the dimensions of care identified by the "Triple Aim." Within the healthscape taxonomy, policy makers ask business-related questions, such as those pertaining to fraud detection,

- How to reduce fraud and abuse by providers?

or operations management,

- How to incentivize providers to invest in technology?
- How to be more collaborative across industry and organizational boundaries?

1 Institute for Healthcare Improvement (IHI). (2016). *The IHI Triple Aim*. Retrieved from http://www.ihi.org/engage/initiatives/tripleaim/pages/default.aspx.

or compliance, and data management and analytics,

- How to encourage the continued movement from a volume-based to a value- and risk-based system?
- How to incentivize providers and payers to leverage analytics and big data most effectively?

Given the impact of policy on patient care, policy makers also ask clinically related questions, such as those pertaining to costs and adherence,

- How to balance quality, cost, and access for patients?
- How to create a more patient-centric system of health care?

or promotion and prevention,

- How to incentivize patients to be preventive?

Regulatory tools for policy makers to impact health care are diverse.[2] Some regulatory tools include the following:

- labeling (disclosure and warning)
- advertising restrictions, taxes (excise duties, value-added taxes, sales taxes)
- product bans or restrictions
- litigation (especially class action litigation)
- self-regulation
- development of educational programs

Examples of policy maker efforts to positively impact patient health include mandatory warning labels on tobacco products to reduce cancer rates, safe driving programs to reduce car accidents, and taxing sugar sweetened beverages (SSBs), such as sodas, to reduce obesity rates. In each example, policy makers make efforts to promote patient health and reduce disease through policy. In this way, policy makers can have a sizable impact on the health-care system at both ends of the healthscape taxonomy, from business to clinical.

PROVIDERS

In an increasingly complex health-care environment, health-care providers and professionals need to save time and serve patients. As a result, health-care providers can be found in all fields of expertise, including medicine,

---

2 Gearhardt, A., Roberts, M., & Ashe, M. (2013). Is sugar is addictive . . . What does it mean for the law? *Journal of Law, Medicine & Ethics, 41*(Suppl), 46–49.

dentistry, psychology, midwifery, nursing and nursing homes, and allied health professions. The far-reaching expertise of providers in the health-care system allows providers to ask questions that extend across the business and clinical ends of the healthscape taxonomy.

Providers ask business-related questions, such as those pertaining to data management and analytics,

- How can analytics and big data be utilized most effectively?

or financial accounting and reporting,

- How to continue doing Medicare and Medicaid in a fiscally responsible manner?

or operations management,

- How can technological advancements be leveraged to enhance quality, improve efficiency, reduce costs, and grow revenue?
- How to be more collaborative across industry and organizational boundaries?

Given the primary role of providers to deliver care to patients, providers also ask clinically related questions, such as those pertaining to data security,

- How to increase data protection and cybersecurity?

or disease management, and health and wellness,

- How to engage in effective population health management?

or costs and adherence,

- How to become better at telehealth, home health care, and community-based care?
- How to create a more patient-centric system of health care?

Providers are thus at the front lines of delivering value in the health-care system by interacting with patients, both directly (e.g., delivering a treatment) and indirectly (e.g., making health information more accessible to patients via flyers and pamphlets). In this way, providers can have a far-reaching impact on the health-care system at both ends of the healthscape taxonomy, from business to clinical.

PHARMACIES

Pharmacies are unique in that they specialize in preparing and dispensing medicines and drugs. Pharmacists are the "drug experts" with advanced cross-disciplinary training in medicine and the biological, physiological, and behavioral sciences.

Pharmacies ask business-related questions, such as those pertaining to data management and analytics,

- How can analytics and big data be utilized most effectively?

or marketing and promotion, and social networking,

- How can the pharmacist continue to be a voice that patients trust?

or operations management, and profitability analysis,

- How to embrace new value-based payment models?
- How to be more collaborative across industry and organizational boundaries?
- How to leverage the growth in specialty medicines?

Given the accessibility of pharmacies to patients, pharmacies also ask clinically related questions, such as those pertaining to clinical assessment,

- How to continue integrating clinical services and retails operations?
  or disease management,

- How can the pharmacist develop a more robust role as a key member of the health-care provider team?

In many ways, pharmacists are the most accessible health-care professionals in that patients do not need an appointment to consult with them. Accessibility is a key part of what generates value in health care. In this way, pharmacies play an important role in generating value in health care at both ends of the healthscape taxonomy, from business to clinical.

PHARMACEUTICALS

Pharmaceutical industries represent a cross section of medicine and the life sciences. These industries mainly create large molecule drugs, small molecule drugs, and medical devices. The biotechnology, medical device, R&D, and pharmaceutical companies that create these drugs and products are vital to the innovative culture of health care. For example, the doubling of the human life expectancy in the twentieth century[3] is largely attributed to the development of medicines and vaccines (i.e., drugs and products) over that time.

Pharmaceutical industries ask business-related questions, such as those pertaining to operations management,

- How to improve the efficiency of the clinical trial process?
- How to be more collaborative across industry and organizational boundaries?

or research and development, and financial accounting,

- How to control drug prices given high R&D costs?
- How to make sure payers reimburse costs for drugs and devices?

With the potential for innovation that can promote better patient care, pharmaceutical industries also ask clinically related questions, such as those pertaining to costs and adherence,

- How to shift from a volume- to a value-driven system?

or disease management,

- How to integrate new products such as biosimilars and personalized medicine?

Pharmaceutical industries are at the forefront of the future of medicine. These companies create and develop the drugs and products being used now and are actively engaged in R&D for innovations to change the future of health care. Such innovations can improve the *quality* of care, *access* to care, and *costs* of care, thereby generating value across the healthscape taxonomy, from business to clinical.

PAYERS

Payers are the organizations and businesses that provide insurance and payment for health-care benefits. Health insurance plans can vary in coverage in terms of the size of deductibles and/or co-payments, options for treatment available to the policyholder, costs of the policy, and flexibility for choosing providers. Health-care expenses can cost well more than what a typical

[3] National Institute on Aging and World Health Organization. (2011). *Global health and aging* (Publication 11–7737). Bethesda, MD: National Institute on Aging.

patient can afford, thereby making payers an essential part of the health-care ecosystem. Payers close the gap between what patients can afford and the actual costs of care.

Payers ask business-related questions, such as those pertaining to data management and analytics,

- How can analytics and big data be most effectively utilized?

or financial accounting/profitability analysis,

- How to accommodate increased consumer demand for transparency (e.g., cost comparison tools, price estimates, billing clarity)?
- How to embrace new value-based payment models?

or operations management,

- How to operate in an era of increased patient fiscal responsibility?
- How to be more collaborative across industry and organizational boundaries?

Given the need for payers to close the gap between what patients can afford and the actual costs of care, payers also ask clinically related questions, such as those pertaining to promotion, prevention, and disease management,

- How to incentivize preventive care by patients and providers?
- How to enhance care coordination?

or costs and adherence,

- How to create a more patient-centric system of health care?
- How to engage in effective population health management?

Payers are an important part of the health-care ecosystem in that they help to offset expenses for patients. The more affordable care is, the more access patients have to the health-care they need. Given the *value* that is created when patient care is made accessible, payers are a vital segment of the health-care system for generating value across the healthscape taxonomy, from business to clinical.

Competencies for Analytics Across the Healthscape

The pentagonal framework of the 6 Ps and the healthscape within which these industries operate is key to establishing processes that integrate analytics as an effective tool for assessing data and guiding decision-making in health care. The effectiveness of analytics across the healthscape taxonomy will be bolstered by collaboration within and between the 6 Ps. More than this, these industries need to achieve basic competencies to be able to utilize analytics as an effective tool for analyzing the vast data sets that HCOs produce every day.

Analytics is like any other decision-making tool: When properly utilized, it can be invaluable; when misused, it can be misleading. To avoid the misuse of analytics, it is critical to identify fundamental competencies for utilizing analytics effectively. While there are many competencies that can bolster the utility of analytics across the healthscape taxonomy within and between the 6 Ps, we can identify five (5) fundamental competencies here:

1. *Industry knowledge*. Before we even look for data, let alone analyze it, we must ask relevant questions. Knowledge of the health-care industry is thus a vital preliminary competency to effectively utilizing analytics.
2. *Data synergy*. "Finding" the data that is needed to make decisions is an important step. Processes need to be in place such that HCOs can readily (a) aggregate the relevant internal and external data, (b) explore or review the data to identify possible omissions, errors, or other anomalies, and (c) disseminate the data in formats arranged for use in analysis or reports.
3. *Analytics knowledge*. The saying, "There is more than one way to skin a cat," coined by Mark Twain, is stated to mean that there is more than one way to get what you want. This is true of analytics, where often there are multiple tools available to you depending on the types of questions being asked and the nature of the data available. Therefore, having a strong understanding of analytics is vital to ensure that the most appropriate tools are utilized to guide decision-making.
4. *Analytics capabilities*. HCOs manage a lot of data, generating and distributing reports and dashboards, for example, to understand business performance. Integrating data within and between the 6 Ps generates vast data sets that can be so large that a standard computer would not be able to open the data file. This is often what is meant by big data. It is therefore vital for HCOs to have a physical infrastructure in place to handle all of that data.
5. *Leadership and decision-making*. Ultimately, HCOs need leaders. Leaders who can act upon the vast amounts of data and analyses generated by analytics models in meaningful ways, thereby delivering recommendations and decisions that can not only create a competitive advantage for the organization, but also drive *value* in health care to increase *quality* of care, *access* to care, and reduce *costs* related to providing care.

HCOs will likely experience problems implementing analytic modeling if they lack any of these core competencies. An organization can certainly make use of analytics in segments of interest on a small scale without mastering all of these skills. However, the systematic, structural implementation of analytics at an organizational, and even an industry level, will require that these core competencies be established. In the chapters that follow we take a closer look at the diverse set of analytical tools available to health-care professionals (Chapter 3), and the preparedness of HCOs to utilize analytics (Chapter 4).

REFERENCES

Gearhardt, A., Roberts, M., & Ashe, M. (2013). Is sugar is addictive . . . What does it mean for the law? *Journal of Law, Medicine & Ethics, 41* (Suppl), 46–49.

Institute for Healthcare Improvement (IHI). (2016). *The IHI Triple Aim.* Retrieved from http://www.ihi.org/engage/initiatives/tripleaim/pages/default.aspx.

National Institute on Aging and World Health Organization. (2011). *Global health and aging* (Publication 11–7737). Bethesda, MD: National Institute on Aging.

Chapter 3

The Statistical Toolbox for Analytics

The Analyst's Statistical "Toolbox"

Making use of analytics can seem overwhelming for professionals who often do not think of themselves as "numbers people." However, analytics actually is designed to make numbers more accessible, sensible, and understandable. Analytics is a tool that can actually simplify decision-making by presenting data in digestible units that can inform decision makers in any category of the healthscape taxonomy on what is likely to be true, what could happen, and what should be done going forward.

The tools used by analysts generally fall within three categories, which were first introduced in Chapter 1:

- *Descriptive Analytics.* The tools utilized with descriptive analytics include visualizing data, frequency distributions, descriptive statistics, probability, data modeling, and some inferential statistics. Descriptive analytics answers, "What is likely true?"
- *Predictive Analytics.* The tools utilized with predictive analytics include the use of regression models, forecasting, data mining, simulations, statistical modeling, and risk analysis. Predictive analytics answers, "What could happen?"
- *Prescriptive Analytics.* The tools utilized with prescriptive analytics include linear, nonlinear, and integer optimization, as well as uncertainty modeling and decision analysis. Predictive analytics answers, "What should we do?"

Figure 3.1 summarizes the core statistical "toolbox" available to analysts. In this chapter, we will break down each of these tools to identify its organizational usefulness to guide decision-making. Implementing many of these statistical tools certainly requires technical expertise. However, decision makers can be empowered by knowing what each tool is, why it is useful, and

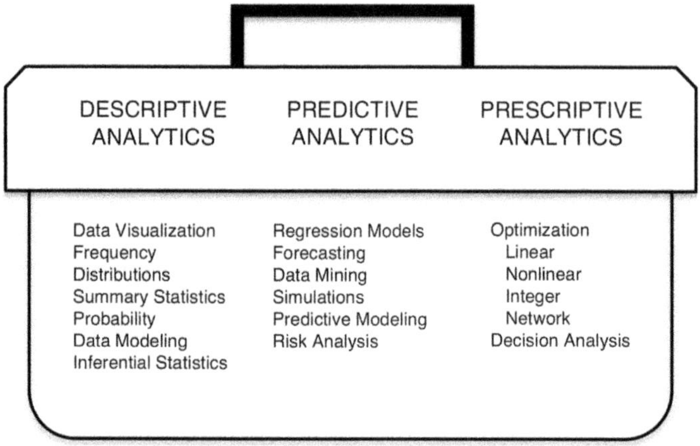

Figure 3.1 The Analyst's Statistical "Toolbox" for Analytics.

what types of questions it can be used to address. For the decision makers, analytics is a tool that helps differentiate their company and outperform their competition. In health care, analytics can answer the marketplace demand for measureable value.

THE "PROCESS" OF ANALYTICS

For business, and across the 6 Ps in health care, analytics has many possible applications. Indeed, analytics is as much an art as it is science. Thoughtfulness, and even creativity, can be advantageous to apply analytics effectively. The "process" of analytics is quite dynamic, largely depending on the types of questions being asked, and the type of data being tested. A general structure for the process, for effective utilization of analytics, requires

- sampling the appropriate data for analysis,
- meaningful organization and preparation of the data for analysis,
- modeling the data for computation using analytics,
- evaluating or assessing the model and its outcomes, and
- making decisions and revising existing models as needed.

At a process level, there are analytics programs available, each of which has its advantages and disadvantages. Some common analytics-based programs include the following:

- CRISP-DM (Cross Industry Standard Process for Data Mining) is a program that organizes the analytics process into six phases:

- ◦ *Business Understanding* (project objectives and requirements; a preliminary plan for analysis)
- ◦ *Data understanding* (initial data collection and exploration)
- ◦ *Data preparation* (data mining and finalizing data set for analysis)
- ◦ *Modeling* (compute analytics model chosen)
- ◦ *Evaluation* (evaluate the model chosen to be certain that it properly achieves the project objectives)
- ◦ *Deployment* (implement model for decision-making; revise as needed)

- SEMMA stands for *Sample* (option step for choosing a subset of data), *Explore* (visual or statistical examination of data), *Modify* (modifications to data, such as data transformations), *Model* (compute the analytics model built), and *Assess* (evaluate the model chosen to assess the validity of the results).[1]
- Six Sigma is a methodology used to improve business processes by utilizing data-based decision analytics models.[2]
- DMAIC is a methodology that when combined with Six Sigma provides an analytics framework for businesses to reduce costs and increase quality. The acronym stands for the five phases of the framework: *Define*, *Measure*, *Analyze*, *Improve*, and *Control*.

SAMPLING AND DATA PARTITIONING

Developing or constructing a model for analysis typically requires dividing or splitting the data set into smaller units or sections. This initial step is typically needed to make pertinent data accessible to "train" a model based on historical or known data.

The process of splitting a data set at random is called data partitioning. Data partitioning is the process of randomly splitting the data into three parts, thereby creating three samples from one larger set. One set is used to build the model (the training set), a second set is used to test it (the test set), and a third set is used to validate the final model (the validation set). The training set is typically used to discover potentially predictive relationships (e.g., do co-pays predict adherence to prenatal care?). The test set is used to assess the strength and utility of a predictive relationship (identified by a range of statistical measures).

Note that a test set is not always needed, in which case the data would be split into only two parts (one for training and one for validation). When a sample is split into training and validation, the convention is for the training set to be a little larger than the validation set (typically a ratio of 60:40)

---

1 To learn more, go to http://www.sas.com.

2 To learn more, go to https://www.6sigma.us/.

because it builds the model. While we would split the data a bit differently if we included the third test set, the data would nonetheless be partitioned such that the training set would be the largest.

One key to data partitioning is to select the samples or "sets" using a random procedure called probability sampling. Probability sampling is illustrated in Figure 3.2. For this procedure, all samples of a given size are equally likely to be selected to ensure that we select a subset of data that is representative of all data from which the samples are selected. Some types of probability sampling procedures that follow the general process given in Figure 3.2[3] are as follows:

- Simple random sampling is a method of sampling data such that all individuals have an equal chance of being selected.
- Systematic sampling is a method of sampling in which the first individual is selected using simple random sampling, and then every *n*th person is systematically selected until all participants have been selected.
- Cluster sampling is a method of sampling in which subgroups or clusters of individuals are identified in a population, and then a portion of clusters that

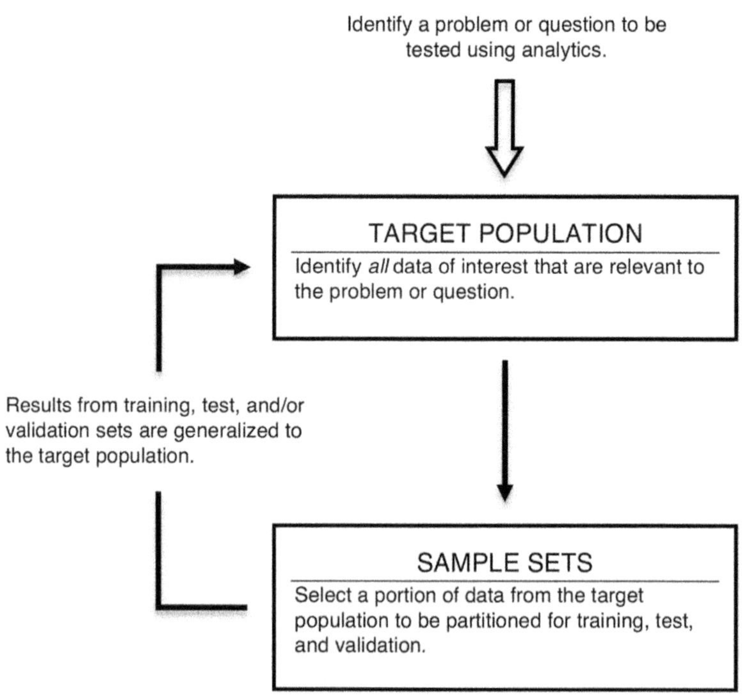

Figure 3.2 The Process of Probability Sampling.

[3] Privitera, G. J. (2017). *Research Methods for the Behavioral Sciences* (2nd ed.). Thousand Oaks, CA: Sage Publications.

are representative of the population are selected such that all individuals in the selected clusters are included in the sample. All clusters that are not selected are omitted from the sample.

- Stratified random sampling is a method of sampling in which a population is divided into subgroups or strata; data are then selected from each subgroup using simple random sampling and are combined into one overall sample.

Often, the key to effective analytics is not necessarily a matter of having technical expertise, which any organization could hire; it is more a matter of having the general "know-how" of the tools available. The remainder of this chapter offers this know-how for each of the three categories of statistical tools identified in Figure 3.1 to empower decision makers in health-care settings.

DESCRIPTIVE ANALYTICS

Descriptive analytics are procedures used to organize and make sense of data, as well as to assess past and current business performance to guide decision-making. An initial step is typically a database query or request for data from a database, which is a structured set of data stored in a computer. Data may be generated in a variety of ways, often returned by Structured Query Language (SQL). This step takes a large data set and simplifies it into digestible units of data that (a) are specifically relevant to what you want to know and (b) can be readily understood and interpreted.

Descriptive analytics comprises a variety of tools and strategies for making sense of data and meaningfully analyzing past and current business performance. Generally, we can break down descriptive analytics into (a) statistics that describe data and (b) statistics that make inferences about data. Let us take a look at each type of statistics.

Describing Data

One aim of descriptive analytics is to simply describe the data we have access to. Descriptive analytics includes many tools used to organize and make sense of data in a way that brings meaning to it. From our statistical toolbox in Figure 3.1, the following tools provide this level of analysis:

- *Data visualization.* Having a list of values in a spreadsheet is often not very meaningful in that it can be difficult to "see" patterns in the data. It is also quite boring. To make the data more presentable and interesting, we can illustrate the data in many ways, such as in graphs, figures, pictograms, charts, and tables. In business, including health care, we often report key performance measures using a dashboard in which the measures are reported in a visual representation, most commonly in figures, charts, and graphs.

Table 3.1 Measures of Central Tendency and Variability

		When to use each measure	
Measure	*Basic description*	*Type of distribution*	*Scale of measurement*
Central tendency			
Mean	The average score in a data set	Normal	Interval, ratio
Median	The middle score in a data set	Skewed	Ordinal
Mode	The most often occurring score	Modal	Nominal
Variability			
Range	The largest minus the smallest score in a data set	Any type of distribution	Ordinal, interval, ratio
Variance	Used to identify "error" in a data set and the size of an observed effect	Any type of distribution	Interval, ratio
Standard deviation	Represents how far scores deviate from the mean in a data set	Any type of distribution	Interval, ratio
Standard error	Reflects "error" between what we expected to observe and what we actually observed	Sampling distribution	Interval, ratio

Table 3.2 Scales of Measurement and Types of Distribution

Category	*Description*	*Examples*
Scale of measurement		
Nominal	Data that represent something or someone	EHR demographic data, such as gender, Social Security numbers
Ordinal	Data that convey order or rank alone	Education level, rankings of regional hospitals
Interval	Data that have no true zero and are distributed in equal units	Temperature, rating scales (e.g., customer satisfaction ratings)
Ratio	Data that have a true zero and are distributed in equal units	Height, weight, age, dollars, hours exercising
Type of distribution		
Normal	A distribution with data that are symmetrically distributed around the mean median, and mode	Distribution for systolic and diastolic blood pressure
Skewed	A distribution with data that includes scores that fall substantially above or below most other scores in a data set	Distribution for household income in the United States
Modal	A distribution of data where one or more scores occur most often or most frequently	Distribution for male/female height (modes occur at different heights)
Sampling Distribution	A distribution of all sample means that could be obtained for samples of a given size	Sampling distribution for mean times to complete surgery

- *Frequency distributions*. One of the common ways in which we identify patterns in data and measure performance is by counting the frequency of times variables occur. For example, we can measure the frequency of car accidents by age of the driver to inform decisions regarding insurance rates for payers, or the frequency of hospital visits per month to inform staffing at a local clinic. Frequency distributions are often reported in a table or in a figure, such as a histogram.
- *Summary statistics*. It is typically advantageous to take a large data set and summarize it using a single value. Summary statistics are individual values that meaningfully represent a data set of any size. Knowing when to use the various summary statistics requires some understanding of scales of measurement and the common types of distributions for data sets. In Table 3.1 we describe summary statistics, and in Table 3.2 we describe the categories for the types of distributions and scales of measurement. In all, there are two categories of summary statistics, as given in Table 3.1:
  - *Central tendency* reflects scores that tend to be at the center of a data set and are used to locate a single score that is meaningfully representative or descriptive of all scores in a data set.
  - *Variability* describes the spread or distribution of the data and reflects measures that help us identify how far scores are spread out in a data set, often from the mean.
- *Probability*. Most decisions in business include some elements of uncertainty (e.g., the "self-life" of a medical device, or turnover among ER nurses), which sets the stage for utilizing probability in decision-making. Probability is the likelihood that an outcome will occur. In health care, for example, we may be interested in profitability (e.g., the likelihood that a medical device will be profitable), survival (e.g., the likelihood that a patient will survive chemotherapy), or diagnosis (the likelihood that a new technology will improve diagnostic accuracy). In each example, probability is used to assess the likelihood of each outcome.

Making Inferences about Data

A second aim of descriptive analytics is to assess past and current performance to guide decision-making. At this level, it really is necessary to take a full course on these analytic strategies to truly utilize them effectively. That said, at a practical level, we can identify what these tools are and how they are useful. From our statistical toolbox in Figure 3.1, the following tools provide this level of analysis:

- *Data modeling*. A common statistical tool is data modeling in which we develop an abstract model that organizes data elements and establishes how they relate to one another and to elements in the real world. Once the model is created, it becomes a visual representation of the nature of the data, how the structure will govern the data, and how the data will be organized or prioritized in the database. The resulting data model, such as a database management system,

- describes the data structure and
- defines the way data are organized in the model.

- *Inferential Statistics.* There is often a need to evaluate specific elements within a data model, and similarly identify statistics that can be used to assess model "fit" in terms of its ability to effectively guide decision-making. There is a family of tests, called inferential statistics, that allows us to take known data in a model and use it to make *inferences* to assess past and current business performance and guide decision-making. The tests available are dynamic in that they often have many uses depending on the types of questions being asked. While the specific tests go beyond the scope of this book, they fall within one of two categories.
  - *Parametric tests* are procedures used to test data with parameters in a population that are normally distributed and measured on an interval or ratio scale of measurement. These are the most common tests because (a) we typically assume that data in a population are normally distributed, and (b) we often measure interval or ratio scale data naturally. Examples of parametric tests are *t* tests, ANOVA (i.e., the *F* tests), and even many of the predictive analyses, such as correlation and regression.
  - *Nonparametric tests* are procedures used to test data with parameters in a population that are unknown or not normally distributed and measured on an ordinal or nominal scale of measurement. While these tests are less common, they are nonetheless effective inferential statistics. Examples of nonparametric tests are the chi-square tests (χ^2) for data on a nominal scale, and for data on an ordinal scale analytics tools include the Mann-Whitney *U* test, the Wilcoxon signed-rank *T* test, and the Kruskal-Wallis *H* test.

PREDICTIVE ANALYTICS

Predictive analytics are techniques used to predict outcomes by examining existing data for patterns or relationships to make inferences forward in time to inform decision-making. Examples of the need for predictive analytics can be found across the 6 Ps. For example, patients may want to predict how co-pays will change so they can afford routine care; policy makers may want to predict the impact of a new law on access to patient care; payers may want to predict the response of different patient segments to an advertising campaign. While details of the analysis tools for predictive analytics go beyond the scope of this book, we can conceptually identify many of these tools here. From our statistical "toolbox" in Figure 3.1, the following tools provide this level of analysis:

- *Regression models.* At the core of predictive analytics is regression analysis, which is a statistical tool used to (a) identify the function that best "fits" the pattern of data (typically linear) and (b) use this function to predict values of one factor, given known values of any number of factors in a data set. A regression analysis produces a line or curve of best "fit" to a data set, which is then used to make predictions. The closer that data points in a data set fall to the best-fitting line or curve, the better the predictions will be.
- *Forecasting.* Predictive analytics is largely built on the need to predict change. Forecasting is an analytical strategy used to estimate or predict change into the future. Change is expected, making it imperative that decision makers be able to forecast (i.e., estimate) future events, such as insurance prices, interest rates, and economic indicators needed for financial planning. A variety of models for forecasting are used in business, such as time series, regression-based models, and analysis of trends.
- *Data mining.* While data mining is a predictive analytical tool, this is a strategy that borrows a lot from descriptive analytics (e.g., data-mining tools to identify patterns in data) to evaluate patterns and features among variables in large data sets, including big data. Data mining uses visualization, summary statistics, and correlation and regression. In health care, the amount of data available is growing exponentially, making data mining techniques an important tool for "mining" through all of that data to guide decision-making.
- *Simulations.* Once a model is developed, it represents the key characteristics or patterns of the data. The model represents a system that can be simulated to represent the operation of the system over time. A simulation, then, is a method for implementing an existing model, statistically or over time, to test how the system that it represents will perform. A commonly applied example of simulations is a Monte Carlo simulation, which is used to replicate system outcomes over many trials to test the distribution of resulting outcomes.
- *Predictive modeling and risk analysis.* At the heart of decision-making in business is prediction, in that leaders in business make decisions looking to the future for expected outcomes. Predictive modeling is a tool used to "peer into the future" by transforming inputs into output data that is used to predict which outputs will occur. We can even build into these models uncertainty, as a way to gauge risk analysis using a variety of analytical tools. A common tool is "what-if" analyses, where we assess *what* could happen in the future, *if* assumptions to the model or model inputs were modified.

PRESCRIPTIVE ANALYTICS

Prescriptive analytics, as illustrated in Figure 1.2 in Chapter 1, is an analytical approach that integrates descriptive and predictive analytics to find the best course of action for a given situation by (a) entering existing data as inputs, and then (b) feeding the outputs back into the system as inputs to update the model. While details of the analysis tools for prescriptive analytics go beyond the scope of this book, we can conceptually identify many of these tools here. From our statistical toolbox in Figure 3.1, the following tools provide this level of analysis:

- *Optimization.* The process of optimization is to select values of *decision variables* (values a model seeks to determine) that minimize or maximize an *object function* (the value we want to maximize or minimize) with appropriate constraints (limitations or restrictions) added to translate the object function and constraints into mathematical expressions that can then be applied to identify optimal solutions to a problem. Developing an optimization model fundamentally consists of four steps:
    - Select the decision variables (e.g., select values for money spent on R&D projects).
    - Identify the object function (e.g., maximize profit and revenue or minimize costs).
    - Add appropriate constraints (e.g., management policy, available resources).
    - Translate the object function and constraints into mathematical expressions (can be linear or nonlinear).
- *Decision analysis.* Analytics can be used to analyze the decision maker and the decision process itself. Decision analysis is unique in that it is utilized to analyze the idiosyncratic preferences people express and their attitudes toward risk that can impact the decisions that they make. This level of analysis provides insights into the decision-making process and techniques for incorporating uncertainty and risk for making decisions.

THINKING OUTSIDE THE BOX: BEING A CRITICAL CONSUMER OF DATA

Derek Walton, Project Manager, Major Projects, Duke Energy Corporation

Analytics is the conduit analysts rely on to transform data into insight. Inferences about any number of factors can be dispelled or supported by empirical data converted into meaningful analysis. With new insight from data I have an advantage that allows me to sharpen my focus on variables that may need a new management strategy. The timeliness of, or the access to, informative analysis can certainly provide competitive advantages and avoid costly or undesirable outcomes. Approaching an analysis with the right questions and an open mind will optimize the benefit it provides. Determining what the right questions are is a critical process on its own and can also be guided by analysis. It is not uncommon at all that in the course of analysis, more significant unidentified problems can surface, either for the problem being analyzed or for a separate issue. This speaks to the importance of allowing data to guide the planning and strategy development process to more efficiently support decision-making.

PUTTING THE ANALYST'S TOOLS TOGETHER

In this chapter, we covered a lot of ground across a large cross-section of the analytics space. Certainly, there are full texts you can purchase that explain greater details for analytics for the topics in this chapter alone. The aim for this chapter was not to make you an expert in analytics. Rather, as stated earlier, while having the technical expertise in analytics is advantageous, it can be just as advantageous to have a general know-how of the tools available to analysts, and to know why and when these tools are useful for guiding decision-making.

By organizing this chapter using the statistical toolbox illustrated in Figure 3.1, you are empowered with an organized framework for understanding the role of analytics in the decision-making process. More than this, the role of descriptive, predictive, and prescriptive analytics is synergistic. Each approach builds upon one another to provide more information to inform decision makers, as illustrated here:

- Descriptive analytics informs *what has happened.* For example, what are turnover rates among surgeons?
- Predictive analytics informs *what could happen.* Given turnover, how many surgeons do we expect to lose in six months? One year?
- Prescriptive analytics informs *what to do about it.* What can be done to reduce turnover and/or meet hiring needs?

For each type of problem or question that is tested, there are many tools available across the descriptive, predictive, and prescriptive approaches. It is therefore important to be considerate in the decision-making process, for health care especially, about how the decisions made using analytics impact *value*.

REFERENCE

Privitera, G. J. (2017). *Research Methods for the Behavioral Sciences* (2nd ed.). Thousand Oaks, CA: Sage Publications.

Chapter 4

Managing Value in Health Care

Adopting a Culture of Analytics

ADOPTING A CULTURE OF DATA ANALYSIS

Data analytics is about innovation and anticipating change. Consider that many of the tools introduced in Chapter 3 are truly about achieving this very ideal. Leadership is so often reflective (on the data we have), yet analytics allows leaders to be anticipatory (of what the data tells us about the future and what we can do about it).

The brilliant physicist Albert Einstein stated, "Not everything that can be counted counts, and not everything that counts can be counted." This highlights an important feature of analytics: Exploring data allows us to count the data that should be counted. In other words, there is so much data available that not utilizing analytics is akin to "leaving money on the table," and this is especially true in health care. Imagine having massive data sets that can inform decision-making but are underutilized simply because analytical tools are not being applied.

It is the incursion of big data (defined in Chapter 2) that has truly tipped the scales toward utilizing analytics in health care. The movement toward a culture of analytics in health care, as in other industries, often involves three stages:

- *Data Collection.* In health care, systems are adopted that specifically support patient workflow and data collection. This stage is characterized by the adoption of EHRs (defined in Chapter 1).
- *Data Sharing.* In health care, there are many independent, yet collectively integrated industries, and thus a need for sharing data across the 6 Ps. This stage is characterized by the creation of health information exchanges

(HIEs) that allow health-care professionals and patients to appropriately access and securely share vital medical information electronically.

- *Data Analytics*. In health care, there is a growing body of big data that, if shared across the 6 Ps, can be used to drive informed innovation and organizational effectiveness. This stage is characterized by the adoption of data warehouses, which are central repositories capable of storing big data and making it accessible for analysis.

Health care is well positioned to utilize data analytics across the 6 Ps. The readily available data, exchanges, and warehouses allow for the collection and sharing of data, which in turn can then be analyzed to leverage data-based models of decision-making. There are certainly industry challenges for adopting analytics, although with the growing development of technologies and big data, analytics is indubitably going to grow with these trends.

READINESS FOR DATA ANALYTICS IN HEALTH CARE

While the 6 Ps are well positioned to utilize data analytics, not all industries are equally well prepared to adopt it. Many models exist to provide meaningful benchmarks that allow organizations to "check" their progress for adopting analytics. In all, there are five core domains that HCOs should strive to attain:

1. scale (of intervention)
2. standardization (of vocabulary)
3. automation (of reporting)
4. receptivity (to innovation)
5. capability (of organizational resources)

Next, we evaluate each of these core domains as they relate to the utility of analytics in health care.

Scale of Intervention

The scale of an intervention largely refers to the level at which the intervention is supported, whether process-based or patient-based. In all, most readiness models tend to include at least three fundamental levels that, amalgamated, comprise analytical utility to achieve personalized medicine (adapted partially from levels provided in the Healthcare Analytics Adoption Model):[1]

[1] Sanders, D., Burton, D. A., & Protti, D. (2016). *The Healthcare Analytics Adoption Model: A Framework and Roadmap*. Health Catalyst. Retrieved from https://www.healthcatalyst.com/white-paper/healthcare-analytics-adoption-model/.

- *Organizational level.* Organizational processes are an important part of patient-centered care in terms of how data are utilized. Processes on both ends of the healthscape taxonomy given in Figure 2.1 in Chapter 2 are important, from those on the business end (e.g., determining diagnosis-based, fixed-fee-per-capita reimbursement models), to the clinical end (e.g., developing collaboration with providers and payers to manage and support patient-centered communication models).
- *Population level.* Population metrics are vital to realize a sustainable data-driven culture of analytics, where organizations engage in "accountable care," that is, they share in the risks and rewards that are tied to patient outcomes. Population health management equates to value-based care. To achieve this level of care requires collaboration across the 6 Ps. For example, utilizing clinical data (e.g., provider) and claims data (e.g., payer) data is vital. Yet, each data point alone does not achieve the appropriate level of depth of information for analysis. Analyzing these clinical and claims data together to assess patient populations is crucial to achieving population health management. If properly utilized across the 6 Ps, this analysis can lead to improved *quality* of care, increased *access* to care, and decreased *costs* associated with patient care.
- *Patient/Clinical level.* Organizational and population levels aim to develop processes and metrics for analyzing data across the 6 Ps. At a patient level, there tends to be a focus on personalized medicine—medical care and treatment that is tailored to the needs of an individual patient. The idea at this level is to utilize patient data across diverse health-care settings to promote wellness, treat illness, and to do so at a minimal cost. HCOs at this level move from health care to health optimization, and thus prescriptive analytics models are highly utilized to achieve this level of care. Examples of interventions at this level include (1) the utilization of low-cost gene sequencing to inform genetic and familial risk and to promote health and wellness, and (2) fee-for-quality rewards to promote pay-for-value financial incentives for disease prevention/health management, thereby moving patients away from high-cost, acute settings to lower-cost outpatient settings and incentivizing health optimization.

As analytics is incorporated as a strategic decision-making tool across the scales of intervention, it is clear that HCOs will realize improved efficiencies. Increased collaborative efforts across the 6 Ps can result in reduced variability in the manner in which care is delivered. This, in turn, can give way to a new culture of "continuously learning HCOs" that utilize analytics to optimize their delivery of patient care.

Standardization of Vocabulary

Well-defined and well-delivered best practice guidelines can improve the replicability and standardization of care, which can in turn reduce costs, such as reducing unnecessary tests and hospitalizations. Strengthening the standardization of vocabulary can provide a platform from which to measure and enhance quality.

Data are units of measurement without meaning per se. Data represent values that have the potential to drive decision-making. However, without a structure for organizing data meaningfully, it cannot be utilized meaningfully. There is consequently a need for a standardized vocabulary by which we can structure and organize data across clinics, care facilities, health-care systems, or even countries to exchange and apply health information in meaningful ways for HCOs and for patients. Key factors to consider when structuring a standardized vocabulary include but are not limited to the following:

- Structuring data entry using a language from novice to expert and even from one practitioner to another, for example, a general family practitioner may record *myocardial infarction* while a surgeon may record *acute anteroseptal myocardial infarction* for the same disease in a patient.
- Identifying formal definitions that support a shared professional understanding across the continuum of care, to include clinicians, sites of care, languages, and systems.
- Delineating relationships between the vocabulary and the context within which concepts are used, that is, delineating how concepts are defined, combined, and used (contextual).
- Creating meaningful concept identifier codes that are nonhierarchical and thus allow for later relocation and/or multiple classification of concepts.
- Incorporating consistency in the structure of concept symbols and definitions such that they have a single, coherent meaning in the vocabulary.
- Avoiding omissions by creating comprehensive processes for timely, formal and unambiguous methods for "plugging gaps" in the vocabulary, as required.

Developing a structured, standardized vocabulary has the potential to reduce variability in care, thereby supporting efforts to improve patient care. Structuring a standardized vocabulary can further promote decision-making in that it can empower HCOs with the wisdom needed to consistently utilize data in meaningful ways. The progression of creating wisdom from data can be understood using the DIKW (Data, Information, Knowledge, Wisdom) framework, which outlines the progression of data utility:[2]

---

[2] Rowley, J. (2007). The wisdom hierarchy: representations of the DIKW hierarchy. *Journal of Information Science, 33*, 163–180.

- *Data.* Standardizing a vocabulary to define and organize data is essential to giving it meaning and value within a context that it will be processed and interpreted.
- *Information.* Aggregating data into digestible or logical units of information makes data aggregates more useful for analysis.
- *Knowledge.* Creating a knowledge base results from the combination of data and the information extrapolated from it to convey an understanding or "accumulated expertise" to a current problem or question.
- *Wisdom.* Attaining wisdom is reflected in the ability to make multidimensional ethical decisions that optimize data in a way that allows decision makers to act diagnostically in any given situation.

Standardizing a vocabulary is vital to the optimal utility of wisdom gained from data, especially when analytics are applied on such a large scale across the 6 Ps. The ultimate aim of standardization efforts is to develop master vocabularies and reference data that are accessible and functional in data warehouses, to include master patient identities, physician identities, and codes for everything from procedures and diagnoses to facilities and departments. Standardized vocabularies enable data governance such that multidisciplinary health-care teams can make queries across the 6 Ps.

Automation of Reporting

Reporting practices in health care are dynamic, especially with the innovative nature of the industry. Analytical tools can aid the consistent, efficient production of reports generated by HCOs for internal and external use. Internal reporting involves collecting data or information for use by an HCO to inform their decision makers and stakeholders in an organization, whereas external reporting involves collecting data or information that is prepared for viewing by the general public or auditors from outside an organization. The content in external reports typically includes only information and data that are considered acceptable for public viewing, such as to consumers or other relevant stakeholders.

Internal and external reporting can be quite different. Larger HCOs typically have both functions to ensure that their records, processes, and reports are examined at regular intervals. Internal reporting is utilized across the 6 Ps for

- managing operational and organizational business practices and risks;
- informing director, management, executive, and board-level oversight; and
- evaluating key performance indicators at all levels of the HCO.

While there is some overlap in data reported for internal and external use, external reports tend to report more macro-level data, and are used across the 6 Ps for

- detailing regulatory, accreditation, and compliance mandates;
- disclosing funding and payer requirements; and
- releasing financials, especially those related to business operations.

Analytics can be utilized to develop reports that are more reliable, consistent, and accurate. Analyses can be performed using data content stored in data warehouses. There should be text query tools that support keyword searches within and across organizational and patient records, are adaptive to the constantly changing requirements of external reporting, and conform to current versions of industry-standard vocabularies. In all, utilizing analytics to evaluate health-care data can streamline internal and external reporting by enhancing

- the consistency of reports generated,
- the ease of maintaining those reports,
- the reliability and validity of the data reported, and
- the availability of reports as needed.

Analytical tools are key to streamlining reporting practices in health care. The value of utilizing analytics for reporting is key to connecting data sources to the decisions made by HCOs thereby ensuring transparency in what is reported.

Receptivity to Innovation

The optimization of analytics in health care can only be realized when analytics methods are used to solve business problems. Advances in technology alone will not optimize the utility of analytics in health care. Indeed, technologies can be expensive and a poor investment if not utilized optimally. Moving forward, HCOs are best positioned to succeed, adapt to change, and generally "get things done" when they understand business challenges (and strengths), then utilize analytics to correspondingly support the business, and ultimately, patients.

A culture of innovation in health care is an environment that encourages creative thinking and advances efforts to cultivate *value* by meaningfully utilizing data to generate processes that can improve the *quality* of patient care, increase *access* to care, and reduce *costs* associated with care. HCOs gain wisdom from utilizing data in meaningful ways that create value on the business end (e.g., economic, political) and the clinical end (e.g., patients) of the healthscape taxonomy.

Cultivating a culture of innovation can be achieved through measured efforts that encourage the use of data to assess not only what is known (descriptive analytics) but also what could happen (predictive analytics), and what can be done to optimize efficient processes and outcomes (prescriptive analytics). In health-care industries across the 6 Ps, a culture of analytics, then, is requisite for cultivating a culture of innovation. In all, an innovative culture shares the following characteristics:

- supports creative thinking
- advances efforts to cultivate data-driven *value*
- shares a set of values and beliefs about the importance of innovation
- integrates process that reinforce innovation
- leverages data to promote an innovative ecosystem

Innovative HCO cultures cultivate a real sense of desire to make things better and actively support new ideas by allocating necessary internal and external resources to help develop and test them. A desire to innovate nurtures a culture of continuous testing and learning—with data being the vital resource that is assessed and analytics being the vital tool from which to extract that resource in meaningful ways.

Capability of Organizational Resources

The capability of an organization to establish readiness for a culture of analytics largely depends on the resources it has to support that culture. The availability of data is not at issue. In health care, data banks are vast with substantial collections of big data that can have powerful impacts on decision-making. The capability of HCOs to utilize big data analytics centers on their ability to

- connect and leverage data stored in data warehouses,
- collaborate across the 6 Ps to share data and coordinate appropriate access to data,
- communicate internal and external reporting utilizing a standardized vocabulary, and
- optimize analytical outputs to advise decision-making across the 6 Ps.

In this way, the capability of organizational resources will be measured by the efficacy of scale of intervention, standardization of vocabulary, automation of reporting, and receptivity to innovation, as described in this chapter.

Effectively harnessing big data will allow organizations across the 6 Ps to extract meaning from vast digital signals across health care, thereby empowering them to collect, collaborate, communicate, and optimize outputs in ways not otherwise possible.

An ultimate advantage of optimization is, of course, utilizing data to adapt to and anticipate change. In this spirit, the "Thinking Outside the Box" feature delves into the utility of analytics as a tool used to adapt to and anticipate change.

THINKING OUTSIDE THE BOX: ADAPTING TO CHANGE

Gail Mayeaux, Executive Director, Universal Primary Care

In primary care, adapting to change and creating a culture that utilizes data to inform care has both been an incremental and a monumental change. Electronic health records have morphed from simply being an electronic version of a paper chart to being a data collection tool. Claims data has become invaluable to understand your patients' total impact as a health-care consumer. Integrating EHRs and claims data using analytics allows for risk stratification and predictive modeling of when and how to provide care. Given the complexity of the health-care industry, the process of data analysis may never be complete and indeed never wholly accurate, but that should be the goal for each piece of the HCO puzzle. Getting there with big data gets us all to the very individual results of better care for more people and at less cost. Otherwise, the industry and each of its pieces are unsustainable.

VALUE MANAGEMENT

From the beginning of this book, we have emphasized *value*. Indeed, the pentagonal framework in Figure 1.1 in Chapter 1 highlights a value-based health-care system that drives value by enhancing quality of care, increasing access to care, and reducing costs associated with care. Analytics is a key driver to manage the value generated. Value management (VM) is an approach used to advance and sustain an appropriate alignment between the results desired by customers and stakeholders on the one hand, and the resources needed to achieve optimal results on the other.

Value can take on a "life" of its own in many ways. This "life cycle" is captured by the *Value Management Lifecycle* developed by the software company SAP, which stands for Systems, Applications, and Products.

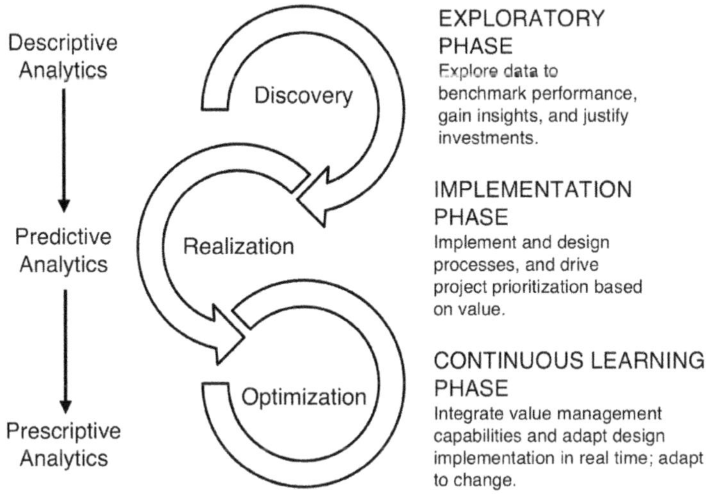

Figure 4.1 Value Management Life Cycle and Analytical Approaches. *Source*: Adapted from SAP Value Lifecycle Manager (https://valuemanagement.sap.com/). Copyright 2017 by SAP.

Figure 4.1 illustrates the nature of this life cycle and overlaps onto it analytical approaches that are applied in health care. Notice that we can readily apply analytics across the value management life cycle using tools readily available in the analytics toolbox illustrated in Figure 3.1 in Chapter 3. As is discussed in Part II of this book (beginning in the next chapter), this overlap between analytics and value management means that industries across the 6 Ps already have the tools they need to translate data into *value* for health care.

The *value* model in health care is about utilizing data to navigate the complexities of the healthscape environment to deliver outcomes that are aligned with strategic goals in a timely and cost-effective manner. From the pentagonal framework identified in Figure 1.1 in Chapter 1, *value* is driven by quality of care, access to care, and costs associated with care. With the value management life cycle in mind, we can look at value management as a catalyst for delivering value. This approach highlights strategies used to improve *value*, which include

- eliminating unnecessary processes (i.e., reducing variability),
- improving resource utilization (e.g., staff, facilities),
- delivering timely optimal processes in the right locations,
- matching clinical resources to parallel clinical process, and
- optimizing costs across the full cycle of care by adopting value-based incentives.

Concomitantly, value management can bolster strategic and organizational goals related to patient care, including

- diagnosing and defining the patient care cycle,
- developing a data collection infrastructure,
- identifying outcomes that matter most to patients,
- mapping the processes of care and associated costs,
- innovating and improving care delivery models, and
- recognizing and overcoming barriers to change.

Value management is increasingly important as a tool for managing change and supporting a health-care culture that is adaptive to change yet still focused on generating value across the 6 Ps. In this way, integrating analytics to leverage value across the 6 Ps is a vital step in the value management model to ensure the viability of the ecosystem of health care.

MANAGING VALUE AND BIG DATA ACROSS THE 6 Ps

As stated in the introduction of this chapter, data analytics is about innovation and anticipating change. The incursion of big data has tipped the scales of management toward utilizing analytics to drive value in health care. Big data is more than just the "size" of data and can vary in many ways, including

- the size, scale, or quantity of data (e.g., EHRs);
- the speed and real-time analysis of streaming data (e.g., real-time alerting using Clinical Decision Support (CDS) software to analyze medical data in real time); and
- the different forms of data (e.g., structured, semi-structured, and unstructured data).

The complexities of big data make the utility of analytical methods essential to uncover the meaning of data in the context within which decisions are made. A health-care culture that shares data should therefore embrace big data strategies and analytics methods. Many vendor options are available (e.g., Microsoft, SAP). Further resources to help organizations identify their readiness for an analytics culture include the following:

- Deloitte Enterprise Value Map, which is designed to identify "practical paths to increase shareholder value."[3]

---

3. See https://www2.deloitte.com/us/en.html.

- DELTA Powered™ Analytics Maturity Model, created by HIMSS Analytics and the International Institute for Analytics (IIA), which provides a functional roadmap to assist HCOs in benchmarking their maturity and progress toward effective use of analytics.[4]

Across the 6 Ps, the health-care ecosystem will benefit most from analysis across the widespread complexity of data—from all data to subsets of data, and from processed data in data warehouses to data analyzed in real time as it is streamed/created. Using a value-based analytics approach in this way shifts the industry culture from an "on-time and on-budget" model to one that is delivered *on par with value*. Therefore, a health-care analytics culture is one where decisions are adopted based on the value they provide; it is an "accountable analytics" approach to health care.

In Part II, we evaluate the 6 Ps starting at the center of the pentagonal framework with patients (Chapter 5), who elect the policy makers (Chapter 6), who then adopt the policies/guidelines for providers (Chapter 7), pharmacies (Chapter 8), and pharmaceuticals (Chapter 9) to follow. At the end of the process, those entities get reimbursed by the payers (Chapter 10). Throughout Part II we will evaluate the role of the 6 Ps from a *patient-centric analytics* approach using the pentagonal framework that was illustrated to open this book.

REFERENCES

Rowley, J. (2007). The wisdom hierarchy: Representations of the DIKW hierarchy. *Journal of Information Science, 33,* 163–180.

Sanders, D., Burton, D. A., & Protti, D. (2016). *The Healthcare Analytics Adoption Model: A Framework and Roadmap*. Health Catalyst. Retrieved from https://www.healthcatalyst.com/white-paper/healthcare-analytics-adoption-model/

---

[4] See http://www.himssanalytics.org/emram/delta.aspx.

Part II

DATA ANALYTICS ACROSS THE 6 Ps

Chapter 5

Data Analytics

Patients

SHIFT FROM PHYSICIAN-CENTRIC TO PATIENT-CENTRIC

An evaluation of the relationship between patients and analytics requires an understanding of its fundamental conundrum: Of all the 6 Ps, patients are most directly impacted by analytics, yet they are generally the least informed regarding data, analytics, and statistics. This is because, historically, the patient has not been thought of as a sophisticated consumer of health information who drives decision-making with regard to his or her own care. Unquestionably, this characterization of the patient is changing.

The multi-trillion dollar health-care industry is undergoing a paradigm shift with the patient/consumer becoming the main user and the end user. The new health market integrates health and wellness, while including a strong retail component. It is shifting from being supply-led to demand-led. HCOs that fail to change in the face of this new reality risk meeting the same fate as other companies that did not respond to changes related to their own products (e.g., Blockbuster and Borders). Patient satisfaction now counts. Perceptions of outcomes can differ between patients and physicians, but treatment decisions are still often shaped more by doctor preferences than by the specific evidence at hand. These are two powerful reasons for giving patient preferences greater weight in the process and access to more data analytics as an essential component of a shared decision-making structure.

Patient-centered care is a relatively new concept, but it can generate clinical, economic, and social gains. Patients have historically played a passive role in the health-care system, even when it came to their own health. In terms of the modern medical era, it has taken about a century for the patient's perspective to shift from being routinely ignored to being lauded as the core of an ideal health-care system. There is an expression that every system is designed perfectly to achieve the results it gets. If that is the case, one is not surprised by the lack of patient centricity in the US health-care system, where structurally, organizationally, and culturally much great emphasis is placed on providers. For example, the preferred time for a patient to schedule a doctor's appointment is between 7 a.m. and 9 a.m., but few clinician's or doctor's offices are open at this time. In this case, the lifestyle and work preferences of physicians take precedence over the convenience of patients.

The patient-centered movement originated from the idea that health-care providers should treat patients as valued human beings with unique physical and psychological needs, instead of as just a bundle of symptoms. Some even use the term "person-centric" in place of "patient-centric" to punctuate the fact that a patient is first and foremost a human being. The driving slogan of the disability rights movement was "nothing about us without us." This is increasingly becoming a norm for the way patients think about their relationship to the health-care system and decisions regarding their individual, personal health.

Because of the information that can be put at the fingertips of patients, technology, data, and analytics are core components of making the health-care system more about "us." Patient centricity has five key elements:

1. whole-person care,
2. support and empowerment,
3. coordination and communication,
4. access, and
5. affordability.

To capture each element, more and more provider organizations are bringing in executives from the retail industry to help with strategy and operations. The differences can be jarring for those coming from outside of health care because of the tendency not to put the customer (i.e., the patient) at the center of everything that has to be done. This new thinking and cross-industry pollination of ideas is crucial to improving the health-care system.

PATIENTS AS CONSUMERS

One of the central transformations in the health-care landscape involves the increasing engagement of patients in their own care. In fact, patients have become so informed and involved that they are often referred to as "customers" or "consumers." Instead of shopping for a new car or leather couch, the patient is seeking the best knee replacement surgeon. As consumers, we are required to make rational judgments regarding which health insurance to purchase, how much financial risk to tolerate, and whether the price of certain services represents value. As patients, we will often be frightened, in pain, and uncertain, which triggers a very different set of norms and values for decision-making.

There is value in differentiating between patients and consumers. Patients are traditionally regarded as anyone receiving medical attention from physicians, nurses, pharmacists, mental health and physical therapists, dentists, and other allied health-care providers. In contrast, consumers are traditionally regarded as people who purchase goods and services for personal use. Patients, by definition, receive care. Consumers, on the other hand, make choices. At any time, only about 15 percent of the US population is in status of being a patient and under some form of care. The other 85 percent of the population is in a consumer or an inactive role. We know that about 5 percent of the population accounts for about 50 percent of all health-care costs.[1] Thus, a relatively small percentage of patients is the driver of annual costs in health care.

The new health consumer is accountable for his or her overall health status and the associated costs. Being an effective health consumer requires attention to several dimensions, which include

- health and wellness
- education
- fitness
- nutrition
- engagement with other consumers, and
- continual learning about options within the health system.

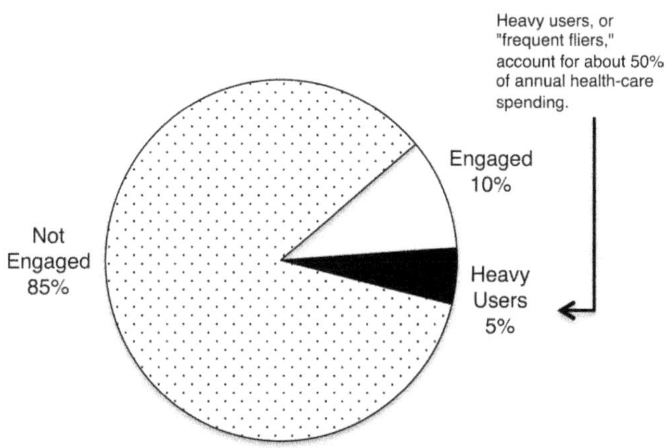

Figure 5.1 Percentages of Health-Care Participants by User Type in US Population.

1 US Department of Health & Human Services. Agency for Healthcare Research and Quality. (2006). *The High Concentration of US Health Care Expenditures.* Research in Action, Issue 19, Rockville, MD. Retrieved from https://archive.ahrq.gov/research/findings/factsheets/costs/expriach/index.html#diff1.

The right recommendation for millions of other patients might be wrong for any given individual. Thus, individual decision-making is essential. As patients increasingly utilize consumer devices and technologies, they are demanding more health information. This will drive another round of connectivity to health-care technology.

Patient engagement at the individual clinical level requires relationship building, information sharing, and shared decision-making, which can be challenging for both the patient and physician. In addition to engaging with the health-care provider, patients must engage with health-care data, information, and technology. The degree, manner, and type of this engagement will likely differ between generations. Some generations of patients are fully wired and plugged-in, and others are interested in innovative technology such as remote monitoring and wearables, which have embedded new forms of data collection and analysis. Many patients today see data as having value, almost as a form of currency. Older generations are very cost-conscious, and they are keenly interested in alternative care services such as retail clinics, telehealth, and other cutting-edge forms of delivery. In this way, many generations of patients are arming themselves with data, information, and analytics and then sharing the results with the rest of the world.

CHALLENGES WITH PATIENTS AS CONSUMERS

As an industry, health care is still lacking clear definitions of the roles and responsibilities for patients in managing their own health. It is crucial that expectations be set that patients regard as feasible and appropriate for them to meet. The ultimate objective of health-care data and analytics is to empower patients to make informed, knowledgeable, and wise decisions about preventive, therapeutic, traditional, experimental, and palliative care options. Patients can be useful in shaping health-care research design and dissemination. At the same time, there is potential for the patient, in the capacity of the consumer, to interfere or become a choke point for the world's most massive industry. For this reason, data information needs to be comprehensible, comprehensive, transparent, reliable, and verifiable.

With current health-care IT systems, there are deficiencies in the ability of patients to utilize existing platforms, most of which were built for very specific, provider-centric purposes. Given that they were not designed for patients, the data embedded in these platforms and the way of presenting it often have limited practical usability for consumers. Even patient portals often present insufficient information because they present the "sick care" picture of the patient rather than the holistic "whole-person" picture. Member portals for health plans can effectively display benefits, deductibles, claims paid, test results, and other basic data points. However, because they were built as business-to-business systems for tracking reimbursable transactions, these systems typically do not speak to a patient's overall health needs.

In addition to software challenges, there are data aggregation and presentation hurdles. Consumer metrics in health care are often inaccessible and underutilized, and when an effort is made to utilize them, they can be chaotic and confusing. For instance, the Centers for Medicare & Medicaid Services (CMS) posts Hospital Consumer Assessment of Healthcare Providers and Systems (HCAHPS) data on the Hospital Compare website, but many prospective patients are unaware that this resource exits. Provider evaluations and ratings are published by various for-profit and nonprofit organizations, including Consumer Reports, Healthgrades, Leapfrog, ProPublica, Truven Health Analytics, and US News & World Report. When choosing a physician or facility, this collection of fragmented information can be synthesized but only by the savviest of consumers. Thus, while there is a sea of data available, only a relatively small subset of it is in a consumable form for the vast majority of patients/consumers.

PATIENT, CONSUMER, AND PERSON

Patient care is not only about patients. As illustrated in Figure 5.2, the "whole being" of an individual consists of multiple dimensions or roles: patient, consumer, and person. The relative weight of these roles varies depending on a variety of factors (e.g., personality, values, income, and state of health), and it can sometimes have cross-purposes. For example, the patient in us can hurt the consumer in us. When a "wonder drug" comes on the market that effectively cures XYZ condition, it might be priced at $1,000 per pill. Given the efficacy of the treatment in this example, the patient in us would naturally ask for this prescription, which would require the consumer in us to pay for it.

Taking a converse example, consumers can sometimes hurt patients. The consumer part of us may resist having the physician take a highly recommended additional X-ray if we will have to pay out of pocket for it, yet that extra diagnostic tool could have revealed a life-threating cancer in the early, highly treatable stages. The growing, undetected cancer would ultimately hurt us as the patient. Finally, in our role as a person, we can hurt both the consumer and the patient part of us. For example, we may resist eating healthy and exercising regularly. Failing to do that will almost inevitably lead to high-cost health problems, including chronic diseases like diabetes, that are expensive and onerous to treat.

We need to focus on the whole human being: consumer, patient, and person. Analytics and technology offer a way forward. If we get patients and

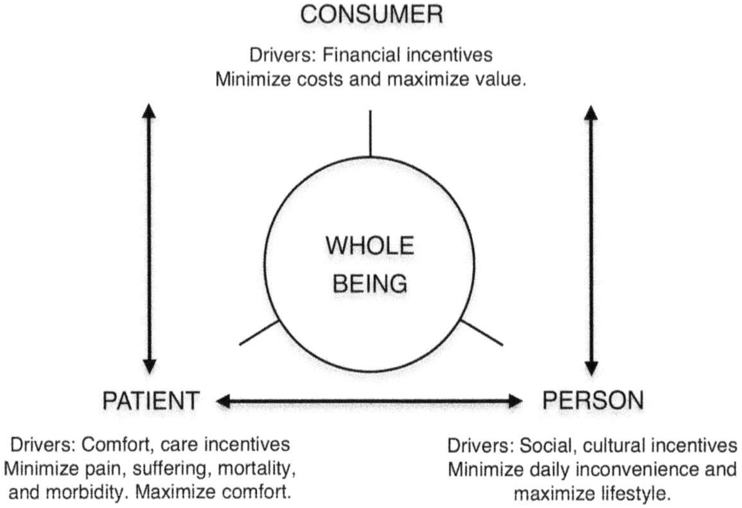

Figure 5.2 The "Whole Being" of Health Care: Integrating the Trinity of Patient, Consumer, and Person to Optimize Incentives for Individual Health.

their families oriented toward the benefits of leveraging technology to gather, organize, and interpret data, the consumer, the patient, and the person will all benefit. The same goes for providers and payers. In the past, we tended to assign payers responsibility for consumer needs and providers responsibility for patient needs. This created friction, with payers castigating physicians for willful indifference to costs, while physicians demonized insurers for being insensitive to the special nature of the provider-patient relationship. We are moving to an environment where addressing both consumers and patients is a shared responsibility.

BENEFITS OF ANALYTICS FOR PATIENTS AS CONSUMERS

In health care, the growth in technology has led to a proliferation of data. To paraphrase E. O. Wilson, the health-care system is drowning in information, while starving for wisdom. There is an emerging wealth of big data being generated by patient-facing technologies such as downloaded apps and sensors worn by patients. In addition, there needs to be a continual effort to harness data from nonclinical sources. Data and analytics can fuel evidence-based decision-making by patients and providers. Many industries improve their performance when customers are provided with appropriate data and analytics to make more transparent decisions. The same is true for health care.

Consumers increasingly crave information whenever they make decisions on purchasing products or services. A significant portion of the modern economy today is driven by search engines offering crowdsourced rater reviews such as TripAdvisor and Yelp. As consumers, we can leverage analytics to search for an in-network provider and research physician and facility background and ratings. Given this, the key becomes providing the consumer with the right information at the right time. The question is how can data be effectively synthesized to yield clear options, generate actionable insights, and hopefully produce wise choices. If done well, analytics can lead to improved self-management of chronic disease (e.g., diabetes and hypertension). Effective patient-centered communication can generate multiple benefits, including lower utilization of high-cost emergency and secondary care services.

Vendors are now emerging to supply more aggregate data for consumers. For example, Amino assembles different categories of data on physicians (e.g., total procedures performed) and has a feature on cost data transparency. Drawing predominantly from social media sources, Crowd Clinical scans for positive and negative comments about provider institutions and then puts that data into a user friendly, digestible form. NarrativeDx created a natural language processing software platform that interprets patient comments and reviews to provide deeper insights into their perceptions. More helpful data, hardware, and software are on the way as we transition to an era of patient as consumer and patient as data analyst.

TOOLS TO SUPPORT ANALYTICS

If the increased reliance upon population health to positively impact quality, cost, and access is to be realized, consumers must be provided with increased technology and analytics. Currently, they have considerably less access to information than medical professionals or benefit managers. However, working together, providers and the leading technology companies are bringing health care closer and closer to the consumer side of society. For example, consumer-facing physician search and rating websites are proliferating, causing many health systems to revamp their Internet presence.

Patients need a platform that aligns their actions and behaviors with incentives and rewards, while also facilitating coordination with various types of population health-care providers, population health managers and health plans. The most patient-centric platforms will create a personalized, data-driven, analytics-rich environment that encompasses the full ecosystem of health, medicine, and wellness. They will also be interoperable with the traditionally more business-centric EHR and insurance benefit platforms.

We need a new type of enterprise platform in health care: a "Consumer-Patient-Person" (CPP) platform. The CPP would integrate benefits information, clinical information, and lifestyle/wellness information. This would put vastly more information in one location for consumers, allowing them to become better gatekeepers of their own health. The CPP platform should transcend sickness and wellness, as well as the roles of patient and consumer, to allow users to successfully navigate their entire health and well-being 24/7 and year-round.

Although patient portals and wearables have increased patient engagement, they do not always generate a shift in overall behavior. To achieve sustainable shifts in health behaviors, we need interoperability to provide patients with rapid and simple access to their entire health and medical history. Without full access to data and sufficient analytics techniques, there is always a danger that patients will treat themselves as just a set of symptoms, which is the key flaw in a provider-centric system.

ANALYTICS AS A DRIVER OF TRANSPARENCY

There has been a change in patient expectations. Health care is now in the box with all the other costs consumers worry about (e.g., food, fuel, college tuition), but unlike most other products and services, health-care consumers do not know prices ahead of time. Moreover, prices can fluctuate wildly from provider to provider. Also, most consumers never have a conversation with their physician about the costs of a visit, a prescription, or a procedure. Because of the lack of information, there is significant anger, frustration, and irritation about health-care prices, with the belief that they are driven by greed. Many customers do not think health-care prices are rational.

In order for pricing tools to work, consumers have to understand how to use the information. Just putting price data out there does not guarantee proper utilization. Many consumers do not associate quality with prices in health care. Given that experts have difficulty defining and measuring quality as well, it is not surprising that many laypeople consumers do also.

New vendors are attempting to fill the gap by offering consumers easier, more transparent ways to comparison shop online among providers. The easy availability of Internet-based medical information (e.g., personal health records) and tools (e.g., apps) has increased the pressure for transparency. The growth in health insurance plans has further stimulated medical consumerism. Transparency in quality and cost information encourages patients to seek out physicians and HCOs providing the greatest value. Infodemiology identifies the capability to systematically locate, aggregate, and analyze user-generated data to inform public health and public policy. In some sense, consumers need to become infodemiologists regarding their own health.

In addition to price transparency, there is now greater focus on quality transparency and assessment of patient experiences. Some HCOs are proactively posting patient ratings of physicians, whether good or bad, on their websites to increase transparency, while aiming to maintain some degree of control and authority. Posting physician ratings can boost an organization's online presence by drawing a significant amount of traffic to its site. If done properly, the system's own ratings can eventually garner a higher Google search rank than commercial ratings sites external to and unaffiliated with the institution. Armed with transparent prices and transparent quality, the consumer is in a considerably stronger position to make health and wellness decisions.

RESOURCES FOR PATIENTS AS CONSUMERS

Information is especially critical for those with chronic conditions, yet these patients often feel the most disempowered by the health-care system. Because of the transparency and empowerment it provides, information can be a great antidote to the feelings of anger and depression that can accompany the search for health-care options. In this regard, a health coach can help with interpreting analytics for patients. The responsibilities of a health coach include working with patients, families, and providers to coordinate care across the continuum. This assistance can enable the most vulnerable consumers to become robust partners in care and to make optimal health decisions.

Vendors are using data analysis to help patients recognize when medical treatment is needed and then preventively intervene to get it scheduled. Or they may detect when a patient fails to refill a prescription. Many concierge medical practices are emerging that enable patients to schedule last-minute appointments on their phones, get certain prescriptions online, and access their medical records electronically. In this way, these private sector vendors serve as data analytics "quarterbacks" for patients and their families.

Primary care providers (PCPs) play an essential role in our health-care system. Strong primary care is the foundation for being able to simultaneously improve the quality of patient care and lower costs. A vital key to patient-centered care is having a primary care system capable of effectively managing the health of patient populations. At the same time, the patient needs to be the coproducer of outcomes. The cooperative model of health care encourages and expects active involvement by all (i.e., patient, family, health coach, providers, payers, etc.). As patients increasingly seek out nontraditional health-care providers (e.g., retail clinics and direct-to-consumer telehealth providers) for more convenient access to care, the cooperative model will need to make room for new actors.

THINKING OUTSIDE THE BOX: PATIENTS

Daniel Yunker, President, Clear Spring Health

Data-driven collaboration and joint venturing are key parts of the future of a more consumer-oriented health care. In order to facilitate the transition to value-based care, providers will need to move patients back to the center of the health-care equation. Analytics, data, infrastructure, and interoperability technologies will be key supporting tools and provide the foundation for providers to form unique joint ventures, partnerships, and/or alliances with other entities. In particular, providers should strive to create value-based joint venture health plans encompassing the full product/service continuum, including commercial group business, direct-to-employer, individual market, managed Medicaid, and Medicare Advantage. To execute on this core patient-centric strategy, providers will need deep expertise, financial capital, and strategic capabilities. And perhaps above all else, in order to optimally serve patients, both payers and providers will be required to effectively leverage data analytics to plan, develop, implement, and assess joint ventures regarding health plans. Health plans and health systems need data, metrics, and measurement to create that continuous positive feedback loop evaluating collaborative ventures, especially the degree to which they (i) increase the centrality of patients and (ii) deliver value, improved quality of care, and better outcomes.

PATIENTS IN THE CENTER AS THE PRINCIPAL 6 Ps

For patients, we examined the fundamental change our health-care system is undergoing from being provider-centric to being patient-centric. Data and technology are both playing a key role in that transition, facilitating greater focus on the needs of patients and consumers. Patient-centered data analytics offers the way forward to improve quality, lower costs, and increase access.

More than ever before, technology generates data that can then be subjected to analytics which serves as the basis for consumers being more preventive and better researchers regarding their own health. This enables patients to become full members of their own health-care teams instead of being passive, sidelined players. Patients are self-motivated, both personally and financially, to take on this more central role because of increasingly high deductibles and coinsurance. The foundation for doing this is greater transparency regarding price and quality, which ultimately translates into increased understanding of value.

REFERENCE

US Department of Health & Human Services. Agency for Healthcare Research and Quality. (2006). The High Concentration of US Health Care Expenditures. Research in Action, Issue 19, Rockville, MD. Retrieved from https://archive.ahrq.gov/research/findings/factsheets/costs/expriach/index.html#diff1.

Chapter 6

Data Analytics

Policy Makers

POLICY AND DATA ANALYTICS

In this chapter, we focus on the utility of data analytics for policy makers. Policy impacts all parts of the health-care industry—from operations to delivery of care. However, it is the place where patients and providers directly interact (i.e., the "point of care") that is the most essential for policy making. We examine how data analytics can inform policy makers and guide data-driven decision-making, particularly in terms of incentives for patients and providers. Key questions regarding patients include how to incentivize prevention and wellness. Key questions regarding providers include how to incentivize increases in quality, decreases in cost (including reduction in fraud and abuse), investment in technology, and adoption of a more patient-centric orientation. The ultimate goal is to help providers balance quality, access, and cost for patients as the system continues to transition from a volume-based to a value- and risk-based system. Analytics and big data can have a significant positive impact, so policy makers should incentivize providers to use them. Moreover, in evaluating providers, policy makers should rely heavily on data.

PATIENT PERSONAL AND FINANCIAL INCENTIVES

Patients often view providers as credible, trusted sources of advice and resources, so based on data, it is natural to reward these providers for positively influencing behavior. Experimental payment models reward providers for maintaining customer health, but where is the reward for the patient? Is the patient payoff purely in the form of better health? The most underutilized resource in our health-care system may be the patients because they have the greatest potential to change their own health. It seems obvious and tautological to say that patients have an outsized potential to positively impact patient health, yet this is sparingly reflected in the framework of financial incentives. Extending payments to patients can increase self-efficacy. Even if patient-directed financial incentives fail to completely change behavior, if they effect some modification, the return on investment can be positive and significant.

The increase in quality and quantity of data facilitates the implementation of personalized incentives. The federal government has authorized grants for states that provide incentives to Medicaid and Medicare beneficiaries to adopt healthy behaviors and join in prevention programs. Any government-promoted programs or initiatives should be evidence based and metric driven. Good target incentives include avoiding early onset diabetes, controlling cholesterol, lowering blood pressure, tobacco cessation, and weight reduction. The starting point is to determine what matters most to consumers. That can be used to build incentive regimes for patients to learn more, take action, and become/stay healthier. This will ultimately lower hospital utilization, particularly the expensive ER visits.

Incentives can substantially improve participation in health promotion initiatives. Rewards can include a yoga mat or a free dental appointment. There are federal regulations providing guidance on using incentives to increase patient engagement with health promotion. Personal incentives can now be customized based on demographics, health records, wearable device data, and expressed prior concerns. The new data can drive valuable insights that providers and payers can leverage to customize incentives to each individual patient, which is likely to increase adherence. The application of these digital health solutions can help patients, providers, and payers focus on specific outcomes.

Financial incentives can take the form of cash rewards, typically relatively small, tied to the patient achieving predetermined milestones. In terms of rewarding behavior, for example, a patient could gain a cash payment for completing an annual checkup or for faithfully adhering to their medications regime. In terms of rewarding clinical outcomes, an obese patient could receive money for losing a certain number of pounds or attaining a specific body mass index (e.g., 22 kg/m2). Diabetics could be rewarded for improving their A1C test scores (e.g., 5.5 percent). A selection of gift cards or certificates can be provided to encourage people to undertake a thorough health assessment, with the card being mailed once the appointment is complete. In order to reward healthy behavior and value-centric utilization, some states provide the reward of a monetary deposit into a health savings account.

There are several data-driven steps for policy makers to take to increase the impact of financial incentives on patient behavior. First, a reward should be of sufficient value to actually motivate behavior. There is no standard incentive that will appeal to all categories of consumers at all times, but generally, the higher one's socioeconomic status, the higher the reward needed to alter behavior. The specific reward could be cash, gift cards, or prizes (e.g., free hotel stay). Second, the intervention should be for a clearly defined period of time, with a skew toward short duration. The longer the required compliance period, the lower the likelihood of overall compliance. Sometimes though short-term satisfaction attainment of goals can be quite beneficial (e.g., a women who succeeds in smoking cessation during her pregnancy, a man who engages in exercise and healthier eating in the wake of heart attack, parents who have their child immunized).

Third, the reward should be provided immediately. For example, if someone loses the target goal of 25 pounds or achieves several consecutive negative tests for drugs, the payoff should be extended right away. Fourth, the objective(s) should be clear and concise. Changing complex behavior, physiological, or physical conditions is difficult. Even skilled physicians may not be confident in what specific course of action a patient should take, so simpler is better for all concerned. Fifth, the objective(s) should be within the control of the consumer. Self-efficacy, even if maximally incentivized and even if the patient is fully responsive, will not positively impact health if patient behavior is orthogonal to those outcomes. Offering as little as $5 or $10 can sometimes be sufficient to motivate healthy behavior, at least for short-term, well-defined objectives.

We have talked mostly about patient rewards, but if a beneficiary fails to pay premiums or complete specified requirements such as health assessments and preventive care appointments, some states impose a penalty (e.g., additional cost-sharing charges) or restrict access to certain extra benefits (e.g., dental or vision). Penalties can include cost sharing, higher premiums, or limits on benefits. Empirically, it is not clear whether restricting primary care as a penalty is more effective than incentives. There is likely some optimal mix of incentives and penalties.

LEVERAGING SOCIAL NETWORKS AND INTRINSIC PATIENT MOTIVATION

Restricting health care to interactions between patients and clinicians is high cost and misses lots of opportunities. One challenge is that providers and payers interact with the patient on a sporadic basis, so the feedback loop can be highly attenuated. Policy makers should promote data-driven experimentation to test the effectiveness of various ways of promoting health in the social domain. We can improve health care by leveraging naturally occurring social dynamics and the power of interpersonal ties. Policy makers should promote innovative structures and the accompanying analytics that help organizations influence the social determinants of health.

Behavior is highly contagious. Family and friends can be free extenders of care. Patients are influenced by how they are perceived and by how others behave. When healthy behavior is made visible, that has a positive impact. Close social relationships (e.g., between spouses) are often very influential on health. All things being equal, if a patient's best friend or spouse eats healthy and regularly exercises, that increases the probability that the patient will too. Social characteristics such as these can be measured and are sources of rich data. In addition, peer intervention can be particularly effective. For example, a weekly phone call between two diabetes patients can provide mutual benefit in their struggles to control blood sugar levels, eat properly, and exercise. Most human beings are responsive to goal setting that is collaborative, community based, and team oriented. For example, two or more people can agree to walk a certain number of steps per week. Any socially oriented collaboration is more likely to work in patient communities that are close or connected, assuming proper metrics and measurements are in place.

When a person is making an everyday wellness decision, such as whether to take a one-mile walk in the park (healthy) or whether to have the late-night high-calorie snack (unhealthy), that person's spouse, family member, or friend is more likely to be present and influence that decision versus a doctor or nurse. The amount of hours patients spend with their clinicians is small compared to the thousands of hours in the rest of their lives. Thus, there should be strategies for incentivizing patients to make healthy decisions in their daily living and collecting data to measure outcomes. Leveraging clinicians for that purpose is expensive. The use of community health and social workers is less expensive and often more effective because those individuals tend to reside in the same communities as the clients they serve. Beyond this, another substantially untapped, relatively inexpensive (and largely free in many cases) resource is the family and friends who are already deeply embedded in the person's life.

If the vast majority of people know that eating well, exercising regularly, and getting annual checkups are conducive to good health, why do so few adopt healthy habits? What seems to be lacking is an intrinsic motivation (i.e., behavior driven by internal rewards). Facilitating the creation of intrinsic motivators is not easy, but the payoff can be significant. Policy makers should encourage people to adopt health goals as intrinsic incentives. Fun can be harnessed for health. Activities that are fun and social can be highly motivating. Social goal setting can also include a competitive dimension. For example, there can be challenge around weight loss or total gym appearances. Chronic diseases such as diabetes, heart failure, and hypertension can be addressed using competition and collaboration. Competition can be stimulated by adherence contests. There can be platforms for peer-support networks. Wellness programs can implement challenges. If a friend, relative, or coworker of a patient is using Fitbit, all things being equal, that patient is more likely to do so too. Many companies are finding that employees with wearable step trackers who get out during breaks to walk together are improving their health, lowering medical costs, and building better relationships with each other.

Technology can facilitate these newer techniques to improve health care, and data is the foundation for the metrics and measures that will be needed to allow patients, providers, payers, and policy makers to assess the effectiveness of social approaches.

GOVERNMENT INITIATIVES TO MOTIVATE PATIENTS

We need comprehensive government initiatives, whether at the local, state, or federal level, that speak to both clinical and social needs while leveraging the greater availability of data. For example, Accountable Communities for Health (ACHs) are innovative institutions that coordinate comprehensive efforts to influence the social determinants of health, particularly in terms of increasing patient self-efficacy. ACHs rely heavily on data to determine what approaches to population health are or are not working. To take another example, state Medicaid programs are experimenting with different approaches for encouraging better behaviors (e.g., annual checkups) and smarter utilization of health services (e.g., avoiding the ER unless entirely necessary) by beneficiaries.

The Medicaid Incentives for Prevention of Chronic Disease (MIPCD) program provided $85 million in grants to states to create patient incentives with rewards including cash, gift cards, points for redeemable health-related products or services, and reduction in cost sharing or premiums. Some of these rewards were given instantly upon satisfaction of the objective and others were redeemable over time. States who participated had to focus on at least one health prevention goal, but several states focused on multiple goals. Examples include the following:

- California created a smoking-cessation counseling hotline and provided participants a $20 gift card to grocery stores and pharmacies.
- Hawaii promoted diabetes testing, education, and self-management initiatives for high-risk individuals with Federally Qualified Health Centers (FQHCs) in the state offering rewards such as cash and gift cards.
- Minnesota provided diabetes prevention and self-management to people enrolled in both Medicare and Medicaid and offered cash rewards for key milestones such as attending the first appointment, achieving weight loss

goals, and completing follow-up visits. To encourage greater participation, the initiative also covered childcare, meals and transportation.

- Texas created flexible spending accounts for beneficiaries with substance abuse or mental health problems who created individual wellness plans including personal health goals.

Some rewards may produce only temporary change and not create a lasting commitment. A person could be incentivized to attend a diabetes prevention class. Other short-term activities include participation in cancer screenings, keeping primary care appointments, calling a tobacco cessation hotline, meeting a high blood pressure reduction benchmark, and getting preventive screenings and routine vaccinations. Long-term objectives such as quitting smoking permanently, maintaining weight loss, and lowering blood sugar levels are more difficult to achieve. While rewards for short-term behavior are generally easier to implement, it is often the modifications in long-term behavior that will deliver the greatest return on investment. As noted above, penalties can also be used in addition to rewards, but the former can be challenging to implement and sometimes can prove counterproductive.

Technology can help with the challenges of implementing rewards (and possibly penalties). Vendors are increasingly competing to offer mobile apps and platforms that engage patients via financial incentives and specific goal setting. People are paid to stay healthy. When people make healthier lifestyle

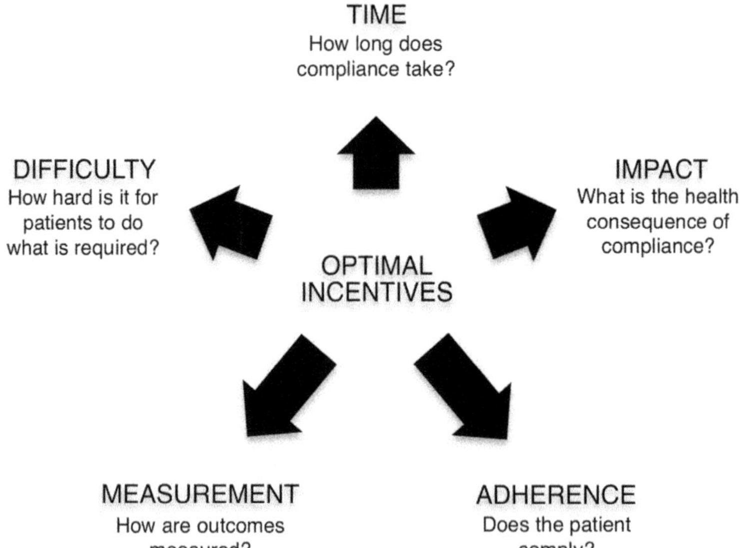

Figure 6.1 Factors that Drive Optimization of Short-Term and Long-Term Objectives.

choices, this usually translates into improved health outcomes and lower costs. For those who are already sick, technology can be used to improve medication and treatment adherence.

PROVIDER INCENTIVES

The United States is struggling with an epidemic in chronic conditions such as heart disease, obesity, and Type 2 diabetes. The current incentive structure contains several points of misalignment. We know the standard fee-for-service (FFS) model incentivizes providers to deliver as many services as possible, regardless of cost or efficacy. This model also does not provide particularly strong incentives for providers to address patient education, clinical coordination, and care fragmentation. With data, metrics, and measurement as the foundation, policy makers increasingly aim to reward physicians who consistently deliver high-quality, cost-effective patient outcomes. It is important to align the incentives of policy makers, providers, and patients to deliver the correct care at the proper price.

The pay-for-performance (PFP) model rewards providers such as physicians, hospitals, and medical groups. When predetermined performance metrics are met (or missed), the provider is rewarded (or penalized). Incentives are typically paid in addition to the standard fee-for-service compensation. Physicians can be incentivized based on attaining specified metrics of quality and cost. Payment adjustments can be made on a per claim basis for certain items and services. A negative payment adjustment can also be applied to physicians and practice groups who fail to report data on certain quality measures. PFP programs generally require strong financial incentives to yield meaningful hospital investments. Policy makers can reward hospitals with bonus payments based on the quality of care they provide. This can be assessed across a variety of quality measures.

Providers are typically evaluated across four big buckets: (1) process—completion of activities and steps presumed to improve patient outcomes; (2) outcome—does patient health actually improve based on provider actions; (3) patient satisfaction—patient self-reported opinion about the quality of care delivery; and (4) structure—equipment, facilities, personnel, and technology used during care. In terms of processes, outcomes, patient satisfaction, and structure, what specifically should policy makers leverage data analytics to measure?

First, any provider bonuses should be based on patient outcomes and costs. Examples of key questions include the following:

- How many patients visit emergency departments for chronic conditions?
- How many patients maintain proper blood pressure and cholesterol levels?

- How many patients self-report leading physically and mentally active lifestyles?
- Of the patients who are diabetics, what portion maintains glucose levels within acceptable ranges?
- Of the patients who are obese, what portion manages to attain medium- and long-term weight loss?

Second, patient satisfaction has taken center stage as a key metric. Via the Hospital Consumer Assessment of Healthcare Providers and Systems (HCAHPS) survey, the Centers for Medicare and Medicaid Services (CMS) now issues public reports on hospital performance as measured by patient-reported experience. Levering the Hospital Value-Based Purchasing program, CMS has forced additional focus on the patient experience by linking Medicare payments to patient self-reports. With regard to these patient experience metrics, hospitals receive rewards based on high absolute rank or improvement over a given time period. There are added incentives for maintaining all metrics above the median. The CMS changes in policy have in turn caused hospitals and other provider organizations to invest in strategies, programs, and initiatives to boost patient experience scores. Patient satisfaction is not a full-proof measure, however, so other assessments are needed.

Third, providers should be incentivized to redesign clinical coordinating roles and patient pathways to improve clinical outcomes and patient satisfaction. In some cases this might include a redesign of organizational structure to improve clinical team effectiveness. Fourth, policy makers should encourage physicians to be concerned with quality and cost issues beyond their own institution or group practice. For example, doctors who make referrals to other doctors with a consistent track record of providing high-quality, cost-effective care can themselves earn bonuses. Fifth, providers should be incentivized to proactively check on patients. A call from a staff member in the near term can prevent or at least ameliorate a problem that would eventually require expensive treatment.

Sixth, we know that mental health has a direct impact on physical health and vice versa. Thus, physicians can be incentivized to ask patients about any mental health problems, including addiction and depression. This helps tie together mental and physical health. Seventh, hospitals can also be provided with financial incentives to reduce unnecessary, unplanned hospital readmissions. This can be focused on certain areas such as acute myocardial infarction, chronic obstructive pulmonary disease, coronary artery bypass graft surgery, elective total hip and/or total knee replacement, heart failure, and pneumonia. Unnecessary readmissions, which are generally very costly, usually result from poor coordination between providers, insufficient discharge planning, and inadequate follow-up with patients.

Better measurement of these metrics will improve the quality of policy maker evaluation of providers. In addition, just as social networking and familial/friend relationships can be used to enhance patient incentives, peer relationships can be used to enhance physician incentives. Peer comparison can be effective in improving quality and cost. For example, in the effort to effectuate voluntary behavior modification, physicians can receive a report contrasting their relatively frequent antibiotic-prescribing habits against stronger performing colleagues (i.e., those who followed the recommended guidelines to prevent overprescribing).

THINKING OUTSIDE THE BOX: POLICY MAKERS

Star* Cunningham, Founder and CEO, 4D Healthware, LLC

Health-care delivery and consumption are at an inflection point. Health-care data analytics has the power to improve the overall experience, engage patients, achieve better outcomes, and reduce costs. The amount of time it takes to realize the value in the data is minuscule when one is only dependent on the technology; in other words, the technology is here to make this happen. The significant time required to bring solutions to market is largely dependent on policy makers and those who are directly responsible for the laws that increase or slow rates of adoption. All stakeholders will benefit from the power of data analytics related to clinical decision support, population health management, and disease monitoring. For these benefits to be realized, policy makers must continually review traditional compliance and regulatory requirements to ensure that policy supports the needs of the most important stakeholder in the health-care ecosystem, the patient.

CHALLENGES FOR POLICY MAKERS

PFP does have several challenges and concerns for policy makers. Here, we identify 12 key challenges and concerns for policy makers to be aware of with regard to utilizing data and analytics to drive decision-making and policy:

1. It can be challenging to measure performance. There should be as clear a link as possible to objectives, metrics, measurement, and outcomes. Quality measures need to be based on robust evidence. If providers perceive that financial rewards are more or less random, that will substantially blunt the impact of incentives.
2. There is a challenge around the size of the financial incentives. The rewards and penalties have to be large enough to materially affect provider

behavior. For example, an incentive bonus has to cover the expenditure of any resources the institution made to generate the improvement plus provide additional profit. A bonus is not a true bonus if it just covers investment costs. Then again, a penalty that is too high may cause counterproductive behavior and place excessive risk on the organization.

3. When viewed as a whole, the numerous studies thus far examining the efficacy of PFP programs show mixed results. Fortunately, there is little to no consistent evidence that PFP has any deep or persistent negative unintended consequence (e.g., current incentives do not seem to increase cost and decrease quality). At the same time, in research on process and outcome measures, there is also no consistency in studies indicating that PFP has large positive impacts on health outcomes. Even if the patient experience, as measured on post-care surveys, improves, that does not necessarily mean the quality of care is improving.
4. There is a danger that PFP initiatives could compromise care access for disadvantaged populations and high-risk patients. Because this pool of patients has complicated medical problems, higher treatment costs, less adherence to treatment plans, and lower probability of recovery, they can be a drag on performance scores. Also, these patients tend to be disproportionately seen by community clinics and safety net hospitals that have very thin margins with little capacity to absorb financial penalties for poor performance. In fact, it could cause these institutions to shut down or at least reduce services to this subpopulation, which would further aggravate the problems of disadvantaged patients.
5. Attribution remains a significant issue because patients often seek care from several providers, including a combination of emergency departments, retail clinics, urgent care clinics, and independent physician practices. This can make it difficult to ascertain who is the patient's primary physician, which is crucial to proper assignment of bonuses and rewards (or penalties).
6. Patient outcomes are ultimately more important than provider processes. However, the latter is typically less difficult to measure and entirely within the control of the provider. In addition to being driven by the quality of care, outcome measures are also a function of key variables such as patient adherence and socioeconomic circumstances.
7. The claims data typically utilized to inform PFP programs are often administrative in nature and lack the detailed clinical information required to make assessments on nuanced patient outcomes.
8. It is difficult to know how to make proper risk adjustments. In terms of severity of illness, socioeconomic status, insurance plan coverage, and a variety of other factors, patients are not created equal. On average, physicians treating patients who present as sicker are likely to retain

an overall client base that is sicker. That is simply a reflection of the base rate rather than an indication that the physician, group practice, or provider institution is underperforming. The health-care ecosystem still lacks a standard validated risk adjustment methodology to account for this data bias.

9. In many ways, health-care providers are drowning in data, so there seems to be too much rather than too little data to analyze. However, when it comes to discerning statistically significant differences between outcomes, there is sometimes insufficient data to make the needed comparisons. Why? Because the sample targeted needs to have enough specificity to be relevant. Aggregating all cases at the level of a health system or group practices produces a large N, but that does not help in evaluating a specific physician. Moreover, comparing results of Physician X's Type 1 diabetes patients to results of Physicians Y's Type 2 diabetes patients is less useful than comparing Type 1's to Type 1's. And comparing all of X's diabetes patients to all of Y's diabetes patients may also not supply the proper distinction we are seeking for measuring certain outcomes. Thus, it can be a challenge to develop sample sizes with sufficient power to identify the statistically significant differences that undergird decisions on rewards and penalties.
10. There can be a high administrative burden attendant to collecting, organizing, and analyzing the data needed for PFP regimes. The amount of time and energy—and hence, financial resources—that providers consume in collecting and submitting data required for quality projects can be significant. Outcome-based clinical measures, as opposed to claims-based process measures, can be particularly onerous to assemble. In fact, because the burden is so high, some providers opt to skip measuring certain performance variables and forgo bonus opportunities.
11. It is often daunting to construct metrics and complete measurement outcomes involving specialty care and ancillary services. Sometimes there is no existing evidence base, or sometimes there is a wide variation in acceptable clinical practice. As a consequence, because metrics and measurement are more tractable, PFP contracts focus on common conditions (e.g., diabetes, hypertension) with strongly validated clinical measures. Yet, specialty care typically involves the most expensive per patient treatment and is a key driver of costs.
12. In order to meet certain incentives, a clinician may need to change their patient workflow, which can be disruptive and counterproductive. Physicians should be included in the negotiations regarding incentives, agree with the standard metrics, see room for improvement, and be willing to invest the necessary time. Without this, offering bonuses may not generate statistically significant improvements in cost or quality.

Policy truly reflects the culture of health care inasmuch as it can impact health-care practices and regulations across the 6 Ps. In this way, being vigilant of the challenges and concerns facing policy makers is vital to ensure optimal utility of data and analytics to drive decision-making and policy.

MAKING AN IMPACT WITH POLICY: BALANCING INCENTIVES WITH METRICS

Even with ample incentives to look after their health, many people still fail to do so. To address this, policy makers should aim to support holistic health initiatives across a wide spectrum of the community. There should be more private sector experimentation and reimbursement innovation. The private sector often mimics the policy prescriptions, including incentives, specified by Medicare and Medicaid. Policy makers should encourage better coordination of care, including increased integration of health, behavioral health, and social services. A key question to ask is how to increase collaboration across industry and organizational boundaries.

Policy makers should continue to actively promote value-based payments as a vehicle for improving the patient experience at hospitals. The key will be to structure those incentives in a way that drives real and enduring improvement. Does a system driven by financial rewards yield a stable commitment to quality, safety, and caring by providers? Evidence is mixed on how much incentives generate meaningful improvements in patient experience. There is an ongoing need to have stronger incentives coupled with more tightly focused metrics and better measurements.

Chapter 7

Data Analytics

Providers

PROVIDERS AND DATA ANALYTICS

In this chapter, we focus on the utility of data analytics for individuals and institutions that are responsible for providing health care at the point of care. Providers are one of the two most important stakeholders in the health-care ecosystem—the other being patients. Because they are on the front lines of care delivery, provider institutions face the continual challenge of balancing quality, access, and cost. We examine how data analytics currently and increasingly will be instrumental in enabling providers to successfully balance these and other competing demands. Key questions include how to optimally leverage data and analytics to be more patient-centric, focus on population health management, stimulate collaboration internally and externally, and establish effective organizational and individual level metrics and measurements.

DATA TRANSFORMING THE PROVIDER ENVIRONMENT

New environmental dynamics are changing the game for the complete care continuum, particularly for providers. Substantial value migration is occurring in the health-care ecosystem with the shift from fee-for-service to outcome-based payments (from volume to value). Providers are heavily impacted as payers increasingly link reimbursement to quality and outcome metrics. The goal of value-based care programs is to generate better outcomes for patients across the care continuum. The shift to value-based reimbursement is reshaping the clinical landscape, financial risk assessment, and revenue cycle management. The health-care market of the future, particularly for providers (e.g., clinics, hospitals, medical centers), will be significantly different from today and in ways we cannot now fully imagine.

Providers are increasingly responsible for the overall outcomes and well-being of a defined patient population. Performing well can mean a financial bonus or share in a savings pool, in addition to avoidance of penalties, for HCOs. Value-based care requires effective population health management and quality reporting. Population health management is an essential competency given the seismic shift in the reimbursement environment. Taking on additional financial risk requires having basic data analytic skill and interoperability capabilities. Providers are targeting processes that will deliver the best return on investment as they transition from volume-based to value-based and as the US health-care system undergoes a data and digital makeover.

Even as budgets are flat or decreasing, big data continues to get bigger and bigger. While providers are drowning in data, they are starving for substance. This is because transforming data into a usable resource requires answers to several challenging questions: What data is available? What format is it in? How can old and new information be synthesized? How can target and acquirer information be integrated? How can we architect electronic information systems in ways that are accessible and understandable for end users? Finally, when it comes to mining data, speed is also an important concern that must be addressed.

The major buckets of data include administrative (provider driven), claims (payer driven), clinical (provider driven), clinical trial (pharmaceuticals driven), social media (patient driven), and wearable technologies (patient driven). Individual level data allow for the more careful tracking of health by patients and providers, and this data can be aggregated and shared once de-identified. Digitization and automated measurement of patient interactions and health outcomes are providing rich data fueling new opportunities for analysis and comparison of contrasting continuum of care interventions. The Internet of Things (IoT) in health care is yielding significant quantities of data on key variables such as dieting habits, exercise routines, physiological parameters, and vital signs. The sheer variety and volume of data is transforming the provider environment.

HCOs are seeking to learn from the pioneering innovations developed by more consumer-friendly industries. Consumer engagement is highly fragmented, spanning all of the Ps as well as some actors outside the health-care system. There is significant information asymmetry between patients and providers. Like so many traditional consumer-oriented businesses, HCOs are striving to develop a detailed mapping of consumer attitudes, interests, needs, and preferences. There are developing consumer data platforms driving analytics and personalized engagement with accuracy, agility, and scalability. Precision analytics requires a holistic 360-degree perspective on patients that is accurate across all internal silos, which will lead to enhanced personalized engagement, better consumer satisfaction, improved clinical outcomes, and higher reimbursement from payers.

In order for a platform to be agile and scalable, there are several criteria. First, it should be able to process any type of data, including structured, unstructured, and semi-structured. Second, the platform should be equipped to handle high volumes and high velocities of data. Third, it should provide an integrated, unified view of the patient without the user having to switch existing source systems. Fourth, it should be able to process data from a variety of sources (e.g., laptops, mobile, streaming data from the web, text notes, and imaging data). The consumer data platform should support personalized engagement at all stages of the patient's journey, with the goal of converting the resulting data into actionable insights that create value for the organization.

The rise of consumerism in health care has created new value streams, and data is the foundational element to understanding these new dynamics. The patient should experience high-touch personalized engagement pre-visit, during visit, and post-visit. Leveraging digital channels and devices, as well as other modalities, the goal is to create a highly personalized journey for the patient with content specific to each stage and pathway of care. High-use channels include email and texting. There has been a rapid growth in consumer-based initiatives. Concierge care, also called direct primary care or subscription medicine, is a growing element of health care. It involves more of a direct relationship between patients and providers, generally giving payers little or no role, which can lower administrative costs. Concierge medicine contains a better alignment of incentives and fewer negative or positive externalities; this new modality of care both generates data and is data driven.

PHYSICIANS, CLINICIANS, AND DATA

Health-care clinicians should be the starting point for thinking about leveraging data. Physicians, nurses, and other point-of-care providers are required to digest a significant volume of information about a patient, arrive at an accurate diagnosis, and then create an effective treatment plan. In recent years, the volume of medical knowledge has exploded, along with growth in the number of diagnostic tests and treatment options. Research studies and other medical information are sometimes contradictory, adding to the decision-making complexity of achieving optimal diagnosis and treatment. Even the best trained, hardest working, most intelligent physicians struggle to keep pace with the latest research and other valid medical knowledge. Due to cost and revenue pressures, physicians are often required to see as many as 50 patients per day and spend as little as 5 minutes with each of them.

The availability of meaningful data and the use of analytics by physicians is a relatively recent development. Data is changing the fundamental nature of what it means to be a physician, as well as producing profound changes in the physician-patient relationship.

HCOs are seeking to create empowered, engaged physicians who leverage actionable analytics to improve outcomes and close gaps on translating best practice models into clinical practice. Decision-making software and statistical analysis, instead of a physician's individual knowledge, can be used to model the best course of action and design treatments for patients. In order to facilitate incorporation of analytics in everyday practice, physicians must have the necessarily tools. The following 6 elements are essential to make analytics most useful for clinicians:

1. *Relevant.* In order to capture the hearts and minds of physicians, the data should speak to how to improve patient outcomes.
2. *Transparent.* Physicians, often skeptical of the trustworthiness of data, need assurances that the data is accurate enough for them to use for their decision-making.
3. *Workable.* The analytics must fit seamlessly into the workflow of the health-care worker (e.g., physician, nurse, care manager).
4. *Comparative.* The data should include comparisons to clinical peers and to industry standards. Physicians are often competitive with each other: "How am I doing compared to Dr. X?" Sometimes the competition is with themselves: "How do I compare to standards of care?" Using data to show physicians the impact of their medical decisions on patient outcomes can serve as a powerful motivator.
5. *Accessible.* To the extent possible, the analytics should include a self-service component. The key is to enable physicians to gain on-demand access to data, so information can be proactively incorporated at the point of care. Physicians want real-time answers to questions on clinical improvement quality. Visualization capabilities can help physicians understand the data.
6. *Supported.* There needs to be proper human and technical support. Physicians are usually not experts in analytics, and they often need assistance in leveraging the data to improve patient care. One technique is to embed data analysts within different departments to provide practice-specific help to physicians on optimizing the adoption and application of analytics at the point of care.

LEVERAGING DATA

Analytics can help optimize clinical workflow, support operations, and provider payment strategies. Population management technology is increasingly popular. HCOs are leveraging descriptive, comparative, and predictive analytics to enhance quality improvement. Descriptive analytics covers individuals and summary data on similarities among groups of patients. Comparative analytics covers differences between groups of patients, including risk stratification and treatment effectiveness. Descriptive and comparative analytics serve as the bases for evidence-based medicine and guidelines. Predicative analytics leverages best practice models, the latest medical research, and existing EHR databases to create predictive models and risk calculations.

While interpretation of results should generally involve human-to-human interaction (e.g., to develop a care management plan based on the data), data can drive clinical decision support. Decision-making support software, powered by complex algorithms, helps physicians identify the patients most at risk for adverse health events, particularly those that are costly. Physicians can then proactively provide treatments and disproportionate preventive attention to those patients. For example, the data can aid in predicting who will likely visit the emergency room or be hospitalized. In a pool of 1,000 diabetics, 50 (i.e., 5 percent) may be the most seriously ill and thus in greatest need of a care management plan to prevent costly emergencies. With an interactive database, physicians can drill down to discover which patients are maintaining their screenings and other preventive services. In turn, organizations can drill down to see which physicians are doing the best job encouraging patients to be preventive and award bonuses accordingly.

Claims data and EHR information can be combined to identify those patients who are sickest and in need of the most care. The system can compare a patient's treatment history with recommended guidelines to discern any variance, and if there was, what consequences that had on outcomes, either positive, neutral, or negative. Software can be used to track patient compliance with medical appointments, filling prescriptions, taking medicine, and following other discharge orders. Data can be used to forecast beds, staffing, supplies, testing, treatment, and other resources. Analytics can help improve operating room efficiencies and patient surgical outcomes. A surgeon can examine how many patients were provided with a thorough prep call or in-person meeting and what specifically they were prepped on. They can also examine differences in outcomes based on different post-op medicines and recovery management recommendations.

THINKING OUTSIDE THE BOX: PROVIDERS

Patrick C. Cunningham, Account Executive, Datica

Enhanced data analytics across the provider spectrum brings forth tremendous promise but with caution. Providers at the point of care are seeing access to new kinds of data sets through a range of digital health services, devices, and amorphous care settings. Inside hospital walls, departments for entrepreneurship and informatics are mining internal data sets for ingenious methods of optimization and emerging modalities of care augmented through historical data paired with increased coordination capabilities. Administrators can provide proactive directives based on thorough analysis of disparate data sets as well as accurate financial modeling on a system-wide basis. As is often the case with increased capabilities, there must be in conjunction, an increase in risk analysis and mitigation. Cloud-based computation and functionality offer tremendous promise for data analytics in care settings but security protocols, compliant networks, and ongoing protective diligence within the larger computational ecosystem are a must to protect the personal data that is most precious.

TOOLS FOR DATA

More data is not always better data, and big data is not always smart data. There are tools available for providers to help make sure bigger data is also smarter data. As detailed below, these tools include semantic analysis, algorithms, artificial intelligence (AI), and machine learning. Some institutions still rely heavily on Excel spreadsheets, different reports in different locations, and other labor-intensive elements. One effective approach is to implement an automated system covering the major care paths of services delivered within the system. The provider can then evaluate each patient encounter in real time. Moreover, as new procedures, techniques, and technologies are brought online, the software can continually assess whether the innovation helps improve patient outcomes. The data-driven gap analysis comparing the target to the reality for every care path will automatically highlight changes that may be needed to enhance quality, cost, and efficiency. In order to lessen the burden of clinical documentation, providers are using natural language processing techniques to generate meaning from free text and static images. As a next step, going beyond mere extraction, providers and vendors are focused on generating sophisticated algorithms that can synthesize the information and convey knowledge. There should be visibility into value, so at the service line level, analytics should provide end-to-end visibility for the full spectrum of care.

The foundational elements for strong analytics include a comprehensive EHR system, an integrated data system, a data lake or data warehouse, and effective routines for continual data cleanup and maintenance. Providers are investing heavily in centralized data warehouses and creation of machine learning models that generate forecasts. Key data-driven tools include algorithms, guidelines, alerts, and scorecards. A data visualization platform can facilitate real-time presentation of data in a form that is easy to comprehend and navigate. It is essential to have a visually intuitive dashboard that can pull from a myriad of data sources, particularly if it permits physicians, nurses, and other clinicians to ask and answer their own questions. From a functional perspective, the package should include alerts/reminders, beneficiary stratification, risk gauging, and other tools that engage point-of-care health workers. In order to effectively predict areas of highest risk and comprehensively track patient activities, the big data needs to be visual. Specialized analytics packages will be needed that convey data in an intuitive, meaningful format. These packages should include clinical analytics algorithms, performance measurement systems, population health management, quality benchmarking, and revenue cycle/claims analytics.

AI and machine learning will bring important expertise into the health-care system to help with the flow, source, and analysis of information. This will be the next major wave for health information technology. Machine learning can be paired with complex algorithms to generate geometric patterns and meaningful clusters from the data, which can then be further analyzed. For example, in many hospitals, typically only heart and vascular service line patients are evaluated for the risk of heart failure and sepsis. However, with a strong system of predictive analytics, a machine learning algorithm can be used to identify and follow up with all high-risk patients. Analytics tools driven by AI and machine learning will bring new players into the health-care sector.

In the health-care sector, there are a large number of potentially significant applications for AI systems. These applications include chronic disease management, clinical decision support, customer/patient service, and enhanced operational efficiency. AI holds the potential to increase personalized patient engagement in health care just as has occurred in other sectors like finance and retail. From a human capital perspective, AI and machine learning hold great potential to reduce human workloads, while improving the accuracy and quality of administrative and clinical decision-making. As the health-care sector moves beyond simply hoarding data, the AI and machine learning service markets are going to grow rapidly, converting big data to smart data.

LEVERAGING ANALYTICS

As health care transitions from fee-for-service revenue models to value-based reimbursement models, providers need sophisticated analytics systems to measure process improvements and track quality metrics. Health-care providers need to have facile understanding of the underlying data and algorithms that yield the analytics to help guide changes in patient and providers actions.

Ideally, the analytics will generate insights that challenge commonly held assumptions regarding

- the fundamental patient-provider relationship,
- the drivers of health and disease, and
- the effectiveness and efficacy of various interventions.

Analytics can improve processes, including daily physician workflow. It can contribute to cost-cutting by allocating internal resources more efficiently, increasing visibility into patient activities, preventing the onset of chronic disease, and reducing unneeded service utilization. Data analytics plays a crucial role in entities like accountable care organizations by exploiting opportunities for preventive care, reducing unnecessary utilization, and improving operational efficiencies.

Given this era of patient attribution to specific providers, one key step is for an organization to leverage analytics to better understand what its population looks like. For example, who is being readmitted today or this week in the population? Who is visiting the ER? Who is failing to adhere to a treatment regimen? Predictive analytics are important, but the first step is understanding the current state of the population. The goal should be to stratify patient clusters and then target those who need and would benefit from an intervention. Successfully identifying a person as high risk does not necessarily mean that risk can be mitigated; follow-up and implementation are essential. The monitoring of patients outside of traditional care settings generates significant additional data regarding chronic disease management, medication adherence, and other interventions. Much of this data collection occurs in the home. Data analytics can also assist with the integration of mental health and physical health to provide more holistic care for patients.

Traditional descriptive statistical models focus on probabilities. Descriptive statistics are excellent for seeing what is in the rearview mirror, but standing alone, they are considerably less useful in looking forward. Predictive analytics can take this a step further, leveraging machine learning techniques to identify, explicate, and then model patterns in the data. Predictive analytics can be used in a variety of administrative, clinical, financial, and operational units. Predictive modeling can help providers understand disease patterns, key treatment trends, and outcome differences. Predictive analytics has a variety of uses, including fraud detection, population health management, and revenue cycle management. Analytics can help predict the future, allowing the organization to be proactive regarding consumer trends.

The rapid growth in predictive analytic systems is being driven by the shift to value-based reimbursement. Predictive analytics is becoming an increasingly necessary element of health care, particularly in terms of improving quality and containing costs. In the age of performance-based reimbursement, correcting a problem "next time" is often too late clinically and financially. Predictive analytics can help bend the cost curve for HCOs and tackle many of an institution's most stubborn quality, cost, and resource-draining challenges. Predictive analytics should be used in cases where change is feasible and would be impactful, enabling providers to move beyond a reactive approach. However, creating an effective predictive analytics culture requires collaboration by the board of directors, senior management, the information technology team, and the clinical experts. Simply because an institution can predict the future does not mean it can or will positively alter the future, particularly given the resource-limited environment of health care. So, one difficult dimension of predictive analytics is making information actionable and then acting on it.

If acted upon properly, predictive analytics can allow physicians to continuously improve treatment effectiveness and help drive tangible, long-term change. Predictive analytics can empower physicians by leveraging an individual's demographic, genetic, medical, and social information to create a more exact patient profile, which is often labeled precision medicine. Predictive tools are not intended to supplant physician judgment. These tools enable physicians to practice more effectively and efficiently. Consider some examples: Rather than only treating a central line infection after it occurs, hospitals can use predictive analytics to prevent potential infections. Real-time predictive analytics facilitates the prediction of which patients have the highest probability of infection and allowing clinicians to intervene proactively. Hospital readmissions is a fertile area for predictive analytics. Predictive analytics can help with avoidable readmissions and staffing needs. A provider can make a prediction regarding which clients would benefit most from having care managers or patient navigators. Based on the results of the predictive analytics, a provider can stage human and physical assets at the optimal clinical and operational points of need. To take another example, based on a patient's history, the provider could anticipate that a patient will need a wheelchair at the point of discharge, removing the typical wait while one is found and thus enhancing the patient experience.

To leverage analytics most effectively, providers must integrate data from as many sources as available and create readily accessible data warehouses. The primary fuel for predictive analytics is data generated by an effective EHR system, which requires streamlining data across locations and platforms. The quality of predictions is strictly a function of the quality of the underlying data. The garbage in/garbage out dynamic is fully applicable. The key is to target the right data rather than trying to analyze all available data; otherwise, the resulting analysis will have reduced or null predictive value. Also, the provider must have and be willing to develop the resources needed to proactively address adverse predictions. In order to close the feedback loop, the clinical results of the interventions based on predictive analytics should be pushed back out into the EHR system.

Predictive analytics is the successor to descriptive analytics. The likely successors to predictive analytics are real-time and precision analytics. Real-time analytics, which is an immediate approach to information sharing, can be contrasted with slower claims-based analytics, which creates lags in predictive modeling. Those lags tend to reduce the accuracy of the predictive analytics. Because most dashboards are backward looking or static, they cannot be used to drive real-time decision-making. Investments in real-time analytics combined with predictive analytics can yield a positive return on investment and contribute to profitability. For example, with emergency room visits, the ER staff can view and immediately leverage information. Building out truly robust real-time and predictive analytics will require collaboration between health providers, payers, and vendors. Precision analytics is an outgrowth of precision or personalized medicine. Precision analytics (i.e., individualized or smart analytics) leverages huge collections of big data to discern the personalized genetic foundations and drivers of diseases such as autism, cancer, and diabetes. Precision analytics includes advanced planning, uniform buy-in (particularly from physicians), and selection of skilled vendors.

SHARING DATA

In theory, the growth in data and technology makes it easier to share patient information. In fact, several barriers have limited the ability of HCOs to share and leverage the power of data externally and internally. Key barriers in exchanging data with other providers include data standards issues, EHR vendor interoperability, and integration shortfalls. Interoperability is obviously central to a network of providers gaining data exchange functionality. The effort to move data between organizations is often subverted by active information blocking, connectivity defects, or data silos. One challenge is that, for valid security, privacy, and competitive reasons, most health systems are unwilling to make their patient information available to physicians and other providers outside their network. Integration and data formatting problems can limit the utility of external information. There is a fundamental fragmentation in the EHR vendor market that gives rise to significant interoperability challenges and unintentional information blocking, which is the inadvertent prevention of data exchange because of long-standing economic, logistical, and technological limitations.

Yet, the business imperative for interoperability is growing. The healthcare marketplace is moving toward having fewer but larger provider organizations. Patients moving among multiple providers will increasingly expect their data to follow them, even if all the providers do not use the same EHR. As the importance of patient attribution grows, providers will need to break down the data silos that are currently preventing information sharing. The data analytics infrastructure should rely on common standards. There should be as much collecting and sharing of data as feasible, with the goal being to achieve seamless data exchange between organizations. This collaboration requires creation of smart partnerships to stimulate development of interorganizational population health management competencies. The system would be stronger if all actors across the complete care continuum would allow all other actors to view their data. Providers should also work with patients, policy makers, and other health-care entities (e.g., pharmaceuticals) to develop best practices and share meaningful insights. This partnering could even extend to increasing interoperability and pooling data in order to strengthen the accuracy of evidence-based care.

The clinical imperative for sharing data is also growing, including adding demographic, lifestyle, and socioeconomic information that reside outside a given provider. Health outcomes are frequently a function of genetic or social determinants that may not be amendable to provider alteration. Relying exclusively on administrative data to develop a risk stratification model can result in low predictive power. A model is only as good as the data sourced. Prescriptive analytics powered by combining clinical data (typically internal) and nonclinical data (typically external) permits more effective patient targeting. Thus, models with information from multiple sources have more predictive power than models dependent on single sourced data. For example, a model of hospital readmissions would be strengthened by the addition of socioeconomic data. Most institutions do not have full information on the patient's lifestyle and other social variables that would be needed to develop full models. Even with sufficient data and reasonably accurate predictions, some cases are so complex that it is difficult to discern exactly when and how to intervene clinically.

Data sharing is often an intraorganizational challenge too, in addition to an interorganizational problem. Providers frequently face challenges with data being siloed in multiple EHR systems that are not interoperable. In many respects, EHRs have not fully realized their potential. Many providers are unable to use any data received electronically from outside sources because there is no capability for integrating it into their EHR system workflows. The difficulties are well documented: convoluted workflows, onerous documentation requirements, and lack of actionable data.

Two key limitations for assessing the right EHR data at the right time are insufficient workflow integration and inconsistent health information exchange. Even when sophisticated integrated delivery networks make a dedicated commitment to achieve interoperability with business partners, data exchange challenges can abound. Providers often times find it challenging to determine how to meet payer demands and which patients will yield the greatest return on investment. Many physician groups do not have the financial and technological expertise to implement the complex EHRs that are needed for achieving higher reimbursements from public and private payers. This is one key driver for merger and acquisition activity between independent group practices and larger health systems. The strong pace of acquisitions has caused a complex amalgam of legacy software, existing workflows, and hybrid infrastructure. Provider consolidation increases the need for internal interoperability regarding acquired and merged institutions.

Within organizations, additional problems include cultural barriers, inherent psychological resistance to change, and traditional organizational and operational structures. In order to develop the actionable insights that drive improvements in metrics, organizations will need to embed interoperability into broader and deeper strategies related to performance and quality. There often is no facile way to integrate big data from external sources into internal big data and daily routines; the data generated by health information exchanges is often not well formatted and organized. This creates a need for a cloud-based analytics platform that can integrate data from across all EHRs and related systems in the provider's information technology infrastructure. A centralized, comprehensive database should include a patient's full medical history (e.g., diagnoses, treatment, and outcomes), risk profiles, and socioeconomic dimensions. Data sharing strategies must evolve as health systems transition to being less dependent on hospital-based acute care and more encompassing of prevention-centric wellness networks.

LEADERSHIP CHALLENGES AND OPPORTUNITIES FOR PROVIDERS

In addition to key analytical, statistical, and technological issues already explored, big data presents leadership challenges and opportunities for those running provider organizations. In these institutions (e.g., hospitals), data has historically been utilized for billing, insurance reimbursement, and clinical research. Slow to digitize and generate meaningful data, the health-care sector, particularly providers, has lagged behind other industries in the adoption of data analytics to drive quality improvement. Many providers continue to struggle with interoperability and the basics of health information exchange. There remains widespread concern by executives about how to effectively leverage big data to enhance patient care, so organizations are investing in developing comprehensive data governance programs. Internal governance processes and structures can promote the production of uniform, high-quality data. It is important to assess the nature and integrity of available information; trusted data is the foundation for informed decision-making. In order to be trusted, data should be valid, reliable, and accessible. Collecting untrusted data with different results from different sources can create more questions than answers.

Data can allow providers to create a branded, personalized connection with consumers, which is increasingly essential given increased marketplace competition. Other industries such as automotive, consumer packaged goods, hospitality, media, travel, and retail have leveraged data on enhanced personalized engagement, but the health-care industry lags behind. The combination of data analytics growth, digital transformation, and rising consumerism has increased patient expectations of engaging, personalized experiences. This represents a fundamental change for the health-care industry. Some provider organizations, including nonprofit health systems, have folded in executives from Amazon, Target, and other retailers to help develop and execute a more consumer-facing strategy. On the whole, with regard to data analytics, the health-care industry lags behind more consumer-oriented businesses like banking, retail, and tourism.

Provider executives need to skillfully manage the change process with individuals, groups, and organizations to implement the data-driven action steps. Talented human capital (e.g., clinical leaders, data scientists, IT experts) is needed to make the bits and bytes, as well as the big picture, of big data meaningful. Providers must invest in their human capital to acquire the competencies needed to become facile users of analytics and optimizers of software, which includes the internal staff (e.g., chief analytics officers, business analysts, data scientists)—or skilled consultants/vendors—who can properly analyze the data. An increasing number of providers have opted to create their own data analytics teams and enterprise systems by hiring experts as full-time staff. Some providers have created a chief data scientist role. When designing data analytics interfaces, it is essential to take into account the needs, preferences, and even frustrations of end users, particularly the systemic challenges that can create bottlenecks and roadblocks. Responding to problems raised by data analytics may require allocation of human capital resources such as care coordinators and social workers.

Raw data by itself cannot generate systematic improvement. Instead, the data has to be converted into meaningful information. There also has to be strong institutional leadership and an innovative culture to follow the consequences of the data wherever it may lead. Providers have to determine how to achieve health at scale, even including highly complex cases across the population. Provider executives have to take a sober, realistic look at their current analytics capabilities. In some cases, a complete massive governance rehabilitation of existing data analytics infrastructure and processes may be required, or sometimes an even more radical rip-and-replace approach may be needed. Data is only a means to an end rather than the end itself. The central question must remain: How can big data analytics improve patient care? Predictive analytics is not effective if key stakeholders are not in agreement with using the information. Providers should be open to going where the data directs, even if the outcome is contrary to expectations or politically sensitive internally.

From the perspective of population health, it is important to predict how demographic shifts can potentially impact utilization. Strategic analytics leadership is crucial. Providers should aim to target and tailor their analytics rather than take a catchall approach. Organizations can leverage analytics as a competitive differentiator. It is important to use analytics throughout the organization. To fully execute on predictive analytics, organizations need improved business intelligence models. It is crucial for key leaders in the organization to commit to a culture of continuous improvement. Integrating analytics into administrative and clinical workflows can be difficult. It is important to have an effective data governance structure and to ensure that there are uniform data definitions across the organization. An effective system should combine clinical/EHR, financial, operational, and pharmacy data.

Chapter 8

Data Analytics

Pharmacies

PHARMACIES AND DATA ANALYTICS

In this chapter, we focus on the utility of data analytics for pharmacists and pharmacies. Medication is a central component of patient care, so by extension, pharmacies—as the principal dispensers of drugs—have a key clinical role. Because medical treatments typically include the patient taking one or more drugs, whether over-the-counter or prescription, this is also an important component of cost. Analytics are helping pharmacists lower costs (e.g., optimizing the supply chain efficiency) and most importantly, improve quality (e.g., flagging opioid abuse, increasing patient adherence, reducing prescription errors). Key questions include how to embrace new value-based payment models, how to integrate clinical services and retail operations, how to continue being a voice that patients trust, and what is the best way to develop a more robust role as a core member of the health-care provider team?

THINKING OUTSIDE THE BOX: PHARMACIES

Matthew Dreckmeier, Clinical Pharmacist, OptumHealth

The pharmacy automation market, which is forecast to exceed $5 billion annual within the next five years, is increasingly important for pharmacies and pharmacists. The rapid growth in this market is attributable to several drivers, including the growing geriatric population, pressures to minimize medication errors, needs for enhanced inventory management, and rising labor costs. Improvements in IT infrastructure, along with the crucial utilization of data and analytics, are robustly expanding the potential of pharmacy automation systems to achieve cost savings and quality improvements. Both inpatient and outpatient pharmacies are levering automation systems to handle routine pharmacy tasks regarding the compounding, dispensing, packaging, retrieval, storage, tracking, and updating of medicines. There are several specific operational coverage areas: automated drug compounding, carousel storage systems, medication dispensing cabinets, packaging and labeling systems, robotic dispensing systems, and tablet splitters. And building on these basic tasks, the future of pharmacy automation will center on leveraging AI, analytics, data, and machine learning to allow pharmacists to become even more predictive and proactive in their decision-making regarding patient care.

CHANGING THE DRUG DISPENSING ENVIRONMENT

Medications are essential for three reasons. First, medications are often a key component of treatment best practices such that poor medication management or insufficient patient adherence can lead to suboptimal outcomes, including increased ER use and more hospitalizations. Medication can play a particularly crucial role in the treatment of certain mental health ailments (e.g., schizophrenia). Second, a significant portion of health-care spending is for drugs, so medication matters for performance-based contracting models. Third, medications help create a direct link to consumers, which is increasingly needed in the era of patient-centric care. Because medications are important, pharmacies and pharmacists are important. As a core component of the health-care ecosystem, pharmacies—much like providers, payers, policy makers, and pharmaceuticals—must react and adapt to the changing landscape. Pharmacies are under continual business pressures (e.g., generic reimbursements, specialty drug costs, bundled payments). Adding to the competitive pressures, there is a growth in alternative site providers such as ambulatory surgery centers, home care, pharmacies, and outpatient mental health.

Given the demands of population health management and value-based reimbursement, it is essential for pharmacies and other health-care entities to find ways to leverage drug and pharmacy data to both lower costs and improve outcomes. Pharmacies come in many forms, including hospital pharmacies, independent community drugstores, large national chains (e.g., CVS, Walgreens), and pharmacies embedded within grocery and one-stop-shopping outlets (e.g., Target, Walmart). Pharmacists work in a diverse array of inpatient and outpatient settings, including ambulatory care facilities, hospitals, R&D centers, and stand-alone pharmacies. In these diverse settings and given diverse roles, pharmacies and pharmacists are all facing significant data challenges and opportunities to one extent or another.

Drug dispensing is a core function for pharmacists. As such, this makes them an essential part of the health-care system and leads to several dispensing related, data-driven benefits pharmacists can provide. First and most fundamentally, they verify medication type and dosage, including consideration of allergic and drug reactions. Pharmacists can help optimize the ability of analytics and technology to track drug interactions and side effects. Second, pharmacists often have to manage multiple, high-cost therapeutic drug regimens, which increases the opportunities for drug interactions. For example, a patient might be afflicted with congestive heart failure, diabetes, and rheumatoid arthritis and thus have prescriptions for multiple medications. As part of the dispensing function, pharmacists can proactively anticipate problems related to a given patient taking several medications. Third, pharmacists can help prevent illegal and improper drug prescriptions. Opioid abuse is one of the leading causes of accidental death in the United States.[1] Much of this is driven by the abuse of legally prescribed opioids. By systematically examining prescribing and purchasing patterns, data analytics can help pharmacists identify those patients who are abusing the system.

USES AND VALUE OF PHARMACY DATA

Thanks to advances in technology, pharmacies are generating and accessing more data than ever. What are some of these key technological developments?

- First, with today's software platforms, physicians can now prescribe and manage patient medications in a completely paperless way.
- Second, prescription authorization requests can now be received in real time.
- Third, there are now apps allowing patients to refill orders using their Apple or Android smartphones.
- Fourth, the automation of data capture and solutions has increased.
- Fifth, radio frequency identification (RFID) technology facilitates access control, document tracking, and real-time inventory management.
- Sixth, there is increasing use of innovative telepharmacy programs.

All of these developments translate into more data, and pharmacies have migrated much of this data to the cloud. The foundation for analytics includes pushing data into the cloud, adopting cloud applications, and creating a data warehouse.

1 Centers for Disease Control and Prevention. (2017). Retrieved from https://www.cdc.gov/drugoverdose/.

There are several ways in which data can be utilized in the pharmacy sector. Data can help convert IoT and sensor data into meaningful lifecycle analysis, detect and prevent cybersecurity threats, develop insights for the pharmacy's marketing campaigns, iterate financial risk models, maximize reimbursement, and increase tracking for regulatory compliance on drug distribution. Perhaps most importantly, analytics can be leveraged for key clinical areas: automating clinical pharmacy protocols, calculating nutritional metrics, diagnosis, discovering duplicate prescriptions, distilling lab results, generating patient pharmacy profiles, and prescription label printing. Analytics can be used to discern drug fraud, waste, and abuse based on prescriptions filled, as well as erroneous prescriptions. Medication administration errors expose the pharmacy to potential civil law suits and government regulatory fines. With a strong database, patients taking recalled or unavailable drugs can be located relatively quickly. Data increases overall auditability and transparency of the pharmacy operations, which is crucial for reducing regulator risk.

To fully leverage all this data, analytics should integrate customer intelligence, cybersecurity, and IoT data. The goal is to drive actionable insights for the pharmacy and its stakeholders. This can be accomplished with cutting-edge technologies combined with a smart data management platform. The pharmacy or its vendor can even create data-driven custom applications. Payers, pharmacies, and pharmacy benefit managers can all benefit from pharmacy analytics.

In order to drive meaningful change in the marketplace, pharmacists will need to view data in its totality. Pharmacies are even developing their own EHR systems, which will facilitate their ability to integrate data from other providers. One future trend in analytics will be the integration of "real-world" data, which is non-experimental data gathered from the patient's actual use of the medication, as well as socioeconomic data such as community conditions, family circumstances, education level, and income level. Data can now be collected from more places and thoughtfully aggregated, so pharmacy data can be combined with and integrated into other healthcare data sets, including those outside the institution. Analytics and data sharing between organizations (e.g., private sector pharmacy with public sector agency) can increase prescription drug monitoring and help track medication abuses. Some of the new sources of data include social factors such as quality of life, days worked, and days missed. This real-world data will also increasingly become real-time, and it opens up the possibility of data being richer, more nuanced, and bigger. Big data has to be managed differently. Because of its size, variety, and complexity, big data requires more expert stewardship, including protection of patient privacy and security.

PHARMACY ANALYTICS

Pharmacists and executives leading pharmacies need historical and real-time data to release the power of analytics. There are clinical, marketing, operational, and supply chain analytics. Specifically, analytics can cover drug claims processing, EHRs, e-prescribing, formulary management, hospital and retail pharmacy dispensing, medication reconciliation, and medication therapy management. Data analytics is essential to effective pharmacy benefit management and pharmacy clinical surveillance, which is essential for improved disease treatment. There are now analytical tools that make drug data accessible and actionable, as well as multiple, powerful analytics techniques that pharmacists can deploy to further leverage their data. Analytics can be used to produce interactive scenario simulation software and comparison tools for risk stratification, along with customizable alerts and reports. Modern analytics techniques (e.g., predictive modeling) can be applied to pharmacy metrics, and pharmacies can leverage AI-driven data analytics and achieve transformational results (e.g., increased medication adherence by patients).

The interactive component of data should be intuitive and user-friendly for pharmacists. The visual component is essential to ensure that analytics are fully impactful. The pharmacy should have a scalable, user-friendly, visual analytics platform that allows for robust self-service and so is not overly reliant on IT staff to extract information and meaning. Fortunately, many cloud-based analytics services allow pharmacies to analyze data and develop actionable insights without needing deep coding or technical expertise. The analytics should fit seamlessly into the workflow. Modern visualization techniques include network graphs and dendrograms, which can improve accuracy and speed in understanding complex relationships. Analytics can use color-coded dashboards to enhance understanding. Point-and-click rapid application designs can increase access and use of data across the organization. Based on reaching certain threshold conditions, the system can provide dashboard alerts and email notices. It is important not to "implement and forget" as regards analytics, so after a certain period, it is useful to recalibrate the approach to pharmacy analytics.

For pharmacists, it is important to pursue risk stratification, predictive analysis, and real-time analysis. Risk stratification leverages "up-front" data that is generated early in patient care. It discerns which pharmacy customers and patients are most at risk. When and where possible, risk stratification leverages prospective clinical data that is collected before treatment. Claims data typically contains significant quantities of useful data, but it often has a lag up to 30 days or longer. The sooner in the process the data can be collected and assessed, the closer the institution can move to real-time analysis. A risk stratification score (e.g., high, medium, low) can guide clinical decision-making and patient monitoring, but a lack of comorbidity data can limit the accuracy of the risk stratification.

The best predictive models are based on large, complete longitudinal drug data sets containing demographic information, risk factors, and outcome information on patients. Predictive modeling can be challenging when patient volumes are small, which is typical for highly specialized diseases. In order to build a robust predictive model, there needs to be sufficient numbers of patients to create three sets. The first set is used for building the model and estimation. The second set is used for testing the model. The third set serves to check the internal validity of the model. The model testing and validation serve to test the sensitivity (i.e., ability to identify true positives) and specificity (i.e., the ability to identify true negatives) of the model.

Predictive modeling is an iterative process, requiring tweaks to the model and its assumptions or sometimes even an overhaul. Sensitivity and specificity frequently behave orthogonally such that, as models are adjusted, they do not necessarily increase or decrease together. After a model is established as predictive and robust, including testing it on subsequent data sets, it can be integrated with clinical pathways to establish a continuous feedback loop for learning. ER visits are a reliable predictor of hospitalization and inpatient care. Chemotherapy toxicity is a leading cause of hospitalization. Many of these cases can be predicted, anticipated, and prevented using clinical data. Weight can be a useful additional variable in predictive analytics. For example, in cancer patients, a large weight loss or significant change in BMI is normally cause for concern, and in diabetes patients, a large weight gain is concerning, suggesting potential for clinical intervention.

PHARMACIST PROVISION OF MEDICAL SERVICES

Traditionally, pharmacists have focused on the operational and technical roles in administering a pharmacy. The primarily clinical role was accurately and safely dispensing medications. Thus, historically, pharmacists have not been viewed as clinical providers, so they were unable to bill for outpatient visits or prescribe drugs. However, their scope of practice is beginning to expand, and some states now recognize pharmacists as providers, reflecting the general trend to cover more of their services. Because of their extensive training and specialty knowledge, pharmacists are well positioned to help deliver high-quality care regarding a number of ailments and diseases (e.g., cancer, diabetes). They can fill some of the increasing need for experienced and knowledgeable health-care practitioners. Clinical pharmacists provide comprehensive medication management and related services to patients in a variety of settings. They work closely with physicians, nurses, and other health professionals. Pharmacy clinical analytics and surveillance can help identify clinical intervention opportunities and optimize drug therapies, particularly for difficult to treat pathogens. Payers often rely heavily on specialty pharmacies to help manage care for patients having complex conditions and rare diseases.

At the organizational level, more and more retail pharmacies are getting into the direct provision of medical services. Retail pharmacies have been growing their care delivery services, moving beyond being pure drug dispensaries. They now offer acute and chronic care, preventive medicine, and telemedicine. The vaccination component is particularly robust; pharmacist-driven recommendations hold the potential to increase vaccination rates. Another area is enhancement of antibiotic stewardship and medication management. Pharmacies can help reduce the growth of antibiotic resistance by identifying cases where antibiotics have no clinical benefit. The future of pharmacies and pharmacists will undoubtedly involve a continued growing role in directly providing clinical and medical services. Pharmacists can help increase the quality, safety, effectiveness, and efficiency of health care.

Pharmacies are moving toward data-driven, technology-infused, coordinated care, so pharmacists are playing an increasing role in clinical decision-making as part of a medical care team. Pharmacy analytics can help identify opportunities for improvement, prioritize next steps, document patient interventions, and benchmark performance across the full continuum of care, and pharmacy operations should be included in the orbit of care coordination. For example, specialty pharmacies are involved in clinical guidelines and quality, data analytics and technology, care management and coordination, and patient outreach and triage; they impact the whole continuum of care. A thorough assessment of care includes medication history and reconciliation, which pharmacists are well versed to complete.

For the continuum of care, it is important to link outpatient pharmacy with inpatient and outpatient medical care. Pharmacists can play a crucial role in recommending, monitoring, and evaluating therapies on behalf of the medical team. Data can promote speed, and stimuli response time is often beneficial in the work of a pharmacist. Real-time analytics allows for reduction in the duration to arrive at the appropriate therapy, and data allows for quicker course corrections. Drug products, especially those for specialty conditions, are often very expensive, so quick interventions for therapies that are not working save money. Because pharmacies are a key potential component in promoting continuity of care, it is important for them to interface with the patient's primary care provider and any specialists. For example, oncology pharmacists are now an essential part of the cancer care team and delivery of care to patients with cancer. Pharmacists can also be valuable members of the informatics team. As part of an informatics team, pharmacists can help build technology interfaces, create drug order sets, develop protocols, and implement computerized order entry.

Given their medical and regulatory expertise, pharmacists are well positioned to assist in the development of evidence-based policies, protocols, and standards. Large pharmacy chains are already involved in clinical decision support and evidence-based care management. Data plays a central role in these evidence-based approaches and is also the fuel for pharmacy predictive analytics. This allows proactive intervention by a pharmacist, as well as provides a suggested course of action.

Pharmacists are one of the most trusted voices in US health care. The core competency of pharmacists is compounding, preparing, and dispensing medications, but pharmacists play a crucial role in educating patients, caregivers, and even other health-care professionals. Effective medication management increases regimen tolerance, decreases adverse events, and improves overall patient outcomes. Ineffective medication management can increase adverse effects such as anemia, anticoagulation, constipation, diarrhea, excessive pain, infection, nausea, and vomiting. Pharmacists are in the best position to monitor both drug-disease and drug-drug adverse interactions. In terms of effective medication management and monitoring adverse reactions, pharmacists can then provide direct counseling to patients.

The failure of patients to consistently adhere to their physician recommended drug regimen is a significant problem in the US health-care system. Nonadherence (i.e., a patient failing to take her or his medicine and fill/refill prescriptions) is a direct contributor to hospital readmissions and other adverse consequences clinically. Pharmacists are the experts in drug prescribing and dispensing, and they can help with medication adherence by patients. The key goal is to keep patients adherent and on their prescribed medications, which will keep them healthier. Continuous medication monitoring and data analytics are useful tools for pharmacists because it shifts the focus to improving patient outcomes rather than simply dispensing.

OPERATIONAL USES FOR DATA ANALYTICS IN THE PHARMACY

From an operational perspective, there are numerous ways pharmacies can use data analytics. At the highest level, pharmacists can help tie value to key metrics such as quality, cost, and outcomes. Pharmacists can help administer the retail and reimbursement processes for medications, including co-pay assistance for patients, discounts from manufacturers, and drug replacement/substitutions. They can interact with providers (e.g., attending physicians) and payers (e.g., health plans) to initiate, transmit, and track drug authorization requests throughout the clinical workflow. Pharmacists can play a role in managing drug shortages, minimizing drug waste, and lowering exposure to hazardous drugs.

In terms of costs, pharmacists can help track medication expenditures. Pharmacists can help reduce drug cost per hospital admission and lower overall readmissions. In terms of process flow, analytics can be used to map workflows, identify inefficiencies, and evaluate staffing levels; they can help flag safety issues and surface areas for process improvement. In terms of logistics, pharmacies are part of the drug supply chain, and pharmacists are knowledgeable about drug supplier issues. Data analytics can be used to help manage inventory, streamline operations, and reduce costs. Given the lengthy R&D and FDA approval process, as well as ongoing compliance requirements, there is an urgent need to achieve large-scale efficiencies in the drug supply chain. It is important to shift from simple product chain to an informed value chain to maintain sufficient inventory. One goal is to increase or maintain service level while decreasing inventory levels, which frees up working capital for deployment elsewhere by the pharmacy. In terms of pricing, the byzantine structure for drug prices has resulted in over 100,000 SKUs, along with more than 600 million price permutations, including various chargebacks, group purchasing deals, and rebates. Pharmacists and analytics can bring order to this drug menu chaos.

Pharmacies are well positioned to be true innovators in health care because they already have a strong retail component. Many pharmacies are well versed in customer-oriented initiatives such as loyalty programs, discount coupons, and expedited service. Because pharmacies have tens of thousands of physical locations across the United States, they are better situated to be a more significant in-person part of how consumers access health care. Pharmacy data can be an excellent way to engage consumers/patients, and analytics can help pharmacies optimize their mix of products to achieve better rebates and incentives. Not only is predictive analytics valuable clinically, but it also can be highly useful in engaging customers. This predictability can be utilized to increase the ability to provide the right products/services at the right time for the right customers. Historically, patients with the same indications were generally provided with similar types and doses of medication. With today's individualized data, including genetic makeup, medication regimes can be tailored to suit the specific patient's profile. Prescribing the right medication can speed recovery time, which lowers expenditures. Data can also lower costs by reducing the number of medications prescribed that would have been ineffective.

Pharmacists can form a valuable part of a drug R&D process, principally during clinical trials. They can collect and evaluate data, manage adverse events, provide education to patients and providers, facilitate informed consent, and serve on institutional review boards. Their expertise in dosing, as well as understanding mixing and the methodology of drug administration, can add significant value to a clinical trial. Because they understand the fundamental characteristics of drugs, pharmacists are central to pharmacogenomics, which is the increasingly important science of how individual variations in the human genome impact clinical responses to medications.

EXECUTIVE AND PROFESSIONAL LEADERSHIP

Pharmacies, along with other HCOs, will need to build, brand, embed, and share data-centric applications to make them more accessible, so the market for innovative pharmacy management products is growing rapidly. Organizations will only realize the full value of their data if they have effective business intelligence and visualization tools. A fully distributed, embedded, and visual analytics approach will best allow the organization to solve its most complex data-oriented challenges. Pharmacies also have a growing need to share data externally with customers, suppliers, vendors, and strategic partners. Pharmacists can be part of the conversation regarding formulary management, regulatory compliance, treatment protocols, and improvement of patient outcomes. In addition to the robust clinical applications, the discoveries from drug data analytics can help generate new revenue streams and lines of business. Data analytics can also be used to estimate the financial impact of adverse drug reactions and side effects.

By education, training, and experience, pharmacists are the medication experts. Every pharmacist licensed in the United States must have a degree in pharmacy and pass national exams covering knowledge of medications and drug laws/regulations. Pharmacy specialists complete postgraduate residency and many years of advanced specialty certification. There are now more clinically oriented residencies and certifications as pharmacists have steadily expanded their scope of practice. In the future, health-care careers will be more data driven. In addition to having an expert grasp of drugs, pharmacy codes and quality descriptions, the next generation of pharmacy college graduates will need a working knowledge of data and business analytics given the new data-driven environment for pharmacists.

REFERENCE

Centers for Disease Control and Prevention. (2017). Retrieved from https://www.cdc.gov/drugoverdose/.

Chapter 9

Data Analytics

Pharmaceuticals

PHARMACEUTICALS AND DATA ANALYTICS

In this chapter, we focus on the utility of data analytics for the pharmaceutical industry. Advanced analytics has progressed past the fad status for biotechnology, medical device, and pharmaceutical organizations. It is now an essential part of the strategy and operations for life science companies. Big data is not just for big pharma as many midsize medical device and drug manufacturers are developing first-rate, in-house analytics capabilities. The key overall goals are to maximize market share, revenue, and profit. Analytics options range from the simple to the sophisticated. Data is the fuel for it all, and as the business ecosystem becomes more wired and connected, the volume of data continues to grow. While the pharmaceutical industry has historically enjoyed relatively high profit margins, it currently faces significant challenges, including the lengthy R&D process, high drug development costs, and controversial drug pricing. Pressing questions include how to control drug prices given high R&D costs, how to improve clinical trial efficiency, how to secure reimbursement, how to be more patient-centric, and how to be more collaborative. Key trends in the pharmaceutical industry include consumerization of health care, consolidation of purchasing power, digitization of health records, and shift in reimbursement paradigms. Pharmaceuticals are under tighter payer and regulatory controls. As health-care spending continues to rise, the market is dictating increased efficiency and measurability. The health-care system overall is under tremendous pressure to deliver more value and generate improved outcomes, and the pharmaceutical industry is experiencing a dramatic transformation to an era of personalized, value-based medicine. There is a strong business imperative for improved and more timely use of data.

TRANSITION AND ADAPTATION FOR PHARMACEUTICALS

Health care is becoming patient-centric. Because of its direct relationship with end users, pharmaceuticals already have expertise in customer retention and direct marketing. Advanced pharmaceutical analytics can increase customer centricity by helping create a specific roadmap for each actual and potential user. Big data can be used to find new customers and engage patients. AI can be used to redefine how an organization interacts with its customers, and an effective system can be designed to drive superior customer experiences. The goal is achieve data-driven customer centricity. There are significant unmet patient needs. Pharmaceuticals need to convert patient-centric analytics and intelligence—gathered from across the clinical care continuum—into transformative treatment strategies. The industry needs to better understand how pharmacologic and non-pharmacologic treatments impact patients and organizations.

The pharmaceutical industry is currently making the transition from traditional analytical capabilities and old legacy technologies to considerably more powerful, sophisticated methodologies and tools for data analysis, yet some life science companies are still using the same information data systems they have had for the past decade or two. They generally can only yield excel spreadsheets or flat files from disparate systems data, which then require subsequent integration by IT staff or analytics teams. This approach provides cumbersome and limited abilities to query, especially regarding specific, real-time business needs. The data available from these traditional systems is often insufficient at best and inaccurate at worst. The pharmaceutical industry is continually upgrading strategies, systems, and processes to meet market demands, and companies are radically altering how they gather and use data to drive key performance indicators in all parts of their value chain. They are increasingly transforming themselves into care management platforms rather than being just the makers of drugs.

In response to regulatory requirements (mostly driven by the FDA), the complexity, cost, and length of clinical trials have grown significantly, which has caused an attending increase in the variety and volume of data. Data presents pharmaceutical companies with an opportunity to improve the drug development process. Big data will eventually lead to big changes in how drugs are discovered, developed, and delivered. Data analytics can enhance and accelerate drug development, improving the value and volume of research endeavors. Data can be used to establish a more streamlined, targeted product development process, and big data can be leveraged by the biopharma industry to achieve potentially revolutionary advances, with the goal being elevation in the overall quality of health care.

THINKING OUTSIDE THE BOX: PHARMACEUTICALS

Sherri Matis-Mitchell, Senior Consultant, Text and Data Analytics, Data Star Insights

Big data has been touted as a big win when it comes to cost savings in life sciences. The vast amount of data generated is expected to grow in the coming years. Mobile and digital technologies expand the walls of laboratories and clinics, resulting in even more data, and there is a growing need for actions and decisions based on that data. Big data carries the burden of noise, so data relevancy is extremely important. We need to have the right data to power analysis. While we rush to collect new data, many have yet to thoroughly examine legacy data. There is a cost savings to mining data from completed studies verses new, but data remains locked up in tables that are difficult to extract. Plus, there is hesitancy to reuse data because of data reinterpretation. Industry has recognized the value in linking data, and the proper context for extracted data is essential. There are examples where novel linkage of data created actionable insights for the bench, clinic, and beyond.

SOURCES AND TYPES OF DATA

There has been an unprecedented, exponential increase in the volume of clinical, financial, and operational information, creating a data deluge. It is important to be able to manage and blend data from multiple sources. The pharmaceutical sector has to collect and integrate data from throughout the health-care ecosystem and translate that into meaningful, actionable insights. Big data includes transactional data (e.g., invoices), social data (e.g., tweets/posts), and machine data (e.g., sensors on a Fitbit). Genomics, next-generation sequencing, and advanced integration methods are producing significant quantities of data. Patient engagement responses are another source of rich data. Unstructured data includes physician notes, pathology reports, and numerous scans and images. It is now possible to link data from several different sources, which substantially enriches the complexity of research questions that can be addressed. Figure 9.1 provides examples for structured, unstructured, and hybrid data (i.e., data that incorporates both structured and unstructured types).

In recent years, pharmaceutical companies have leveraged EHRs and insurance claims data. The anonymized version of this data is used to build clinical and scientific models on drugs. The identified version of the data is used to recruit for clinical trials. Claims data can be paired with the clinical data to conduct cost-benefit analyses on the relationship between

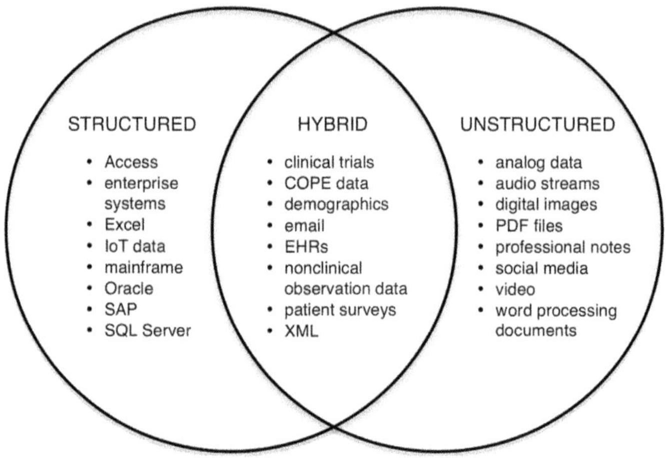

Figure 9.1 Structured, Unstructured, and Hybrid Data.

medications, expenditures, and outcomes. For example, a set of historical data on real-world patients can be analyzed to see how different patient types responded to different treatment approaches. This can be used to discern how clinical outcomes are impacted by the interaction of biomarker alterations, treatment regimes, and individual differences. This approach is particularly useful for indications (e.g., rare diseases, neuroscience impairment) where drug development can be challenging because of shallow patient pools and complex clinical trial processes.

Traditionally, clinical trial protocols were structured to answer well-defined questions regarding a drug's efficacy and safety. The resulting data sets were relatively clean and contained few missing values. This kind of data is a good fit for Statistical Analysis System (SAS) programmers hired by the pharmaceutical industry to efficiently conduct standardized analyses. Real-world data can be drawn from a variety of courses, including EHRs, insurance claims, patient surveys, and social media traffic. It can be leveraged to map out disease patterns, progression rates, and treatment responses. However, real-world data is considerably messier. It often contains a mix of structured and unstructured data, comes in a variety of formats, and includes missing values. Moreover, the data often includes a lot of statistical noise because of biases, inconsistencies, or data entry errors. Analysis of these types of data sets requires considerably more creativity and sophistication. There are real-world challenges (e.g., drug adherence, health-care access) that do not arise in the highly controlled setting of clinical trials.

Much of the data for the pharmaceutical industry, as noted, traditionally originated in clinical trials. This data is robust because that experimental environment is so tightly controlled scientifically. Because of exclusion criteria, many patients are not eligible for clinical trials (e.g., children, comorbid, elderly). Market utilization of drugs does not have these limitations, so the resulting nonexperimental data includes a considerably wider variety of patients, which can enrich the analysis. Observational research is one approach for gathering more clinical data with fewer resources. The pharmaceutical sector can gain access to the generally comprehensive EHR patient data gathered in real time by providers in uncontrolled nonexperimental real-world settings. This can be leveraged to gain a better understanding of clinical outcomes, disease permutations, and treatment patterns. The changing competitive landscape is increasing the need to leverage real-world evidence, which can loop back to help increase efficacy of the drug discovery process. There is a vast amount of real-world, post-approval data that can be a complement rather than a replacement for controlled clinical trial data.

It is important to capture and integrate data, but it is difficult to de-silo information to enable use of data from multiple settings. Historically, data has resided in disparate silos that were often inaccessible and non-interoperable. Archaic collection, storage, and reporting processes limit the ability to leverage data. Pharmaceutical companies are developing a more effective, efficient way of moving data across the enterprise. To address silo issues, to the extent possible, data should be collected and stored in a central depository. However, bigger is not necessarily better. The ultimate key is to access the right data—not all data per se—and to shift data from silos to analysts and executives. The strategic business objectives of the organization should drive the data collection and collation process because shareable data leads to more robust AI and machine learning, which ultimately can lead to better decisions and then better outcomes.

BIG PHARMA USES OF BIG DATA

Big data and AI can help identify solutions, design strategies, and accelerate implementation. Data can help track both actions and outcomes. Data also presents an excellent revenue generation opportunity by helping shorten cycle times, drive rapid change, and increase market differentiation. Data can assist in drug discovery, R&D, patient access, marketing, and reimbursement. One goal for pharmaceuticals is to accelerate financial results; analytics can be leveraged to develop and understand optimal strategic direction, enhance value proposition, increase differentiation from competitors, and allocate budget and other resources. Data can inform marketing and sales campaign development and implementation; it can generate foresight regarding key market trends. Clinically, the applications for data analytics include analyzing genetic conditions, automating portions of the clinical trial process, discovering new indications for approved drugs, identifying diagnoses, and speeding up clinical trial subject recruitment. In the area of oncology, next-generation sequencing data can be leveraged to help diagnose and treat tumors and immune system difficulties. Generating clean and comprehensive compliance data should be prioritized as a practice throughout the entire reporting cycle, not just immediately before submission. In sum, data can generate insights in several areas: business development, brand management, compliance, customer acquisition, customer engagement, finance, go-to-market planning, market research, medical, sales, and sales operations. Pharmaceuticals must continually balance investment in innovation with reducing costs.

Big data, advanced analytics, and AI are foundations for future sales and marketing operating models. The key is to develop advanced analytics tools that will improve customer engagement, marketing efficiencies, and sales force effectiveness. The primary marketing components include prelaunch marketing, customer segmentation, and analysis of sales force effectiveness. The initial months of a go-to-market strategy are crucial in reaching the key stakeholders for pharmaceuticals: patients, physicians, and payers. From a marketing and sales perspective, the applications include brand positioning, identifying specific physicians for outreach, message optimization, personalizing customer interactions, precision targeting of individuals or segments, and understanding market structure. Analytics can also help in understanding the optimal structure for sales representatives. This includes several questions: What should be the size and composition of the internal sales team? How should they be compensated and incentivized? How should they be trained? Where should they be distributed? What are the pros and cons of using a contract sales organization to replace an internal sales force? As part of this, pharmaceutical companies have to weigh targeting physicians versus a direct-to-consumer approach.

Physicians remain the most important stakeholder for pharmaceuticals, so one prominent issue is how to optimally reach this segment. For example, the success of physician outreach strategy is a function of several variables, including the mode of outreach (e.g., call, email, or in-person), the content (e.g., what script is used for phone calls), and various individual level characteristics of the physician (e.g., income levels of their patients, volume of drug prescriptions, and geographic location). Often, thoughtful targeting of a relatively small percentage of physicians can yield the majority of the positive results. Both the content and the mode of delivery should be tailored to fit doctors. Among the key questions analytics can help answer are the following: Which physicians should we target? Who are the best professionals to use for doing the outreach (e.g., sales representative, medical liaison, or fellow physician)? What are the best modalities (e.g., email, in-person, phone)?

Many of these key questions can be explored on an experimental basis, including leveraging data analytics. Testing involves trying a new strategy with a subset of markets, sales representatives, physicians, and consumers. This allows the company to optimize an approach before doing a full rollout. This minimizes the risk of incorrectly investing substantial resources.

Social listening can provide significant data. Whether the potential of translating this raw data into actionable insights is realized depends in part on effectiveness of the analysis. AI can also help in this process by automating learning. Key items to be learned from social listening include brand mentions, trending topics, identity of influential authors, sentiment analysis, and changes over time. There then needs to be a link created between this and the ultimate impact upon the product in terms of brand and sales. Companies need to gain an understanding of the direct causal relationship between digital and social media activities and the brand results.

DATA PRIVACY, SECURITY, TRUST, AND PRESENTATION

Data should be ingested into a central platform. Some data is in third-party vendor systems, so the organization may not be fully aware of what data it does or does not have and how to access it. One first step is to take a data inventory. Data is increasingly kept in the cloud, which typically has advanced security standards. One end goal should be getting the proper data in the right format and location. The garbage in/garbage out maxim certainly applies to pharmaceutical data. Data often contain numerous errors. Contaminated or "dirty" data can lead to erroneous analyses and conclusions. Thus, before use, data should be thoroughly cleaned (e.g., duplicate or erroneous entries removed). Data needs to be collected, cleaned, processed, integrated, and analyzed. In order for data to be trusted, its provenance must be known and trusted. Per the Health Insurance Portability and Accountability Act (HIPAA), identified data is considered protected health information. The de-identification of data involves the removal of all potentially identifying fields like name and address. If data is entered and sorted properly into an intuitive, robust system, analytics becomes much more feasible. To avoid the garbage in/garbage out model, the source data for machine learning must be based on high-quality, reliable data. Any AI-based system will only learn effectively and deliver good decisions/recommendations if it is based on large volumes of quality data delivered in a consistent, standardized format.

The pharmaceutical industry needs data scientists to examine the cleanliness and structure of data to assess its usefulness. If there are many missing values or erroneous entries, the prejudicial effect of the data may outweigh the probative value. Data scientists have powerful techniques to deal with troublesome data. Some organizations even divide the analytics team: One group focuses solely on validly sourcing and cleansing the data while another focuses on analysis and reporting. For example, members of the former group can program algorithms that replace missing data with informed estimates. They also have tests to identify and remove a certain level of erroneous data. Data security should be audited to ensure security. Third-party audits can be used to verify compliance, privacy, and security controls.

Advanced pharmaceutical analytics should be based on curated information and presented in a visually intuitive manner. Visualization should facilitate keen insights and intuitive interpretation. Data analytics should include real-time query and data retrieval functions, and dashboards can be fully integrated with other applications and customizable reports. Charts, diagrams, and graphs facilitate understanding. Despite the increased complexity of the data and the analysis, the results must still be presented to stakeholders (e.g., senior executives, FDA officials, providers) in a way that is intuitive and easy to understand. One overriding goal of pharmaceuticals is to leverage the clinical trial process to ask and answer the right research questions that will ultimately lead to getting the right medicines/therapies to the right patients.

HUMAN CAPITAL AND TECHNOLOGICAL TOOLS

Pharmaceuticals have been investing in big data infrastructure and interpretive tools, as well as securing strategic partners with analytics expertise (e.g., universities, technology firms). Humans are still a key part of the process and must handle building the IT infrastructure, identifying relevant data sources, cleansing the data, building algorithms, and training the AI model to learn. More than ever, the pharmaceutical industry needs analysts and data scientists who can leverage a full range of sophisticated analytical methodologies, technologies, and techniques. The industry has been actively recruiting the requisite human capital, but this remains a significant challenge as pharmaceuticals work to hire and retain data experts. Effective data analysis requires pairing deep domain knowledge of the pharmaceutical industry with data science expertise. The best data scientists are able to create and code customized algorithms focused on the organization's specific data sets and strategic/operational goals. They need strong skills in coding, deep learning, fuzzy logic, and machine learning, along with expertise in AI.

Data analysis in life science companies now requires more collaboration, creativity, and flexibility. Analysts in pharmaceuticals must comprehensively grasp the health-care context for real-world data collection—including any potential biases—and understand how that data can be utilized to address clinical research questions. Data scientists and informaticians are needed to understand the data at a granular level. Internally, many of the top biotechnology and pharmaceutical companies have a major data science practice. Externally, vendors should have a global footprint, industry knowledge, passion for analytics, and technical capabilities. Looking at the human capital needs of the industry as a whole, there are probably not enough skilled, well-trained experts who understand both big data and its applications to the pharmaceutical industry. So, the substantial potential of big data analytics is limited by challenges regarding capacity development and human capital resourcing.

The rapid proliferation of technology has increased the ability to collect and store data. The use of advanced analytical tools, AI, bioinformatics, cognitive computing, machine learning, and mathematical modeling is increasing. There are now platforms that can view, interpret, and summarize billions of patient records in mere seconds. The Internet of things (IoT) is a key source of data, including smartphones, sensors, and wearables that can deliver continuous, real-time information. The key functions of AI include pattern recognition, signal detection, probability estimation, and decision support. AI platforms can assimilate trillions of data points in seconds, work together with big data platforms, and integrate structured data (e.g., spreadsheet) or unstructured data (e.g., social media video). AI and big data platforms can help deliver better products to the market and do so faster. Yet, technology is an enabler rather than a panacea, so AI analytics should be continually developed and refined. The ability of machines to analyze data and pursue basic reasoning is growing. Machine learning can help convert the unknown into the known.

PHARMACEUTICAL EXECUTIVES AND EFFECTIVE DECISION-MAKING

Leaders of pharmaceutical companies often lack the data they need to make highly informed decisions. Why? Sometimes the data is simply not collected. Other times, the organization has the data, but it is not readily accessible. Or if it can be accessed, there may be insufficient human capital expertise needed to effectively interpret data and present it in a way that is visually intuitive. Even today, many reports lack the essential data needed to make decisions. Given the rapidly evolving health-care environment, executives need the ability to quickly test their ideas to see what will or will not work. This design and test approach is the best pathway to optimize the portfolio of marketing investments.

More and more decisions can be automated. AI should sit on top of the IT infrastructure and big data platform; it should drive analysis and recommended actions based on the data. The one-size-fits-all approach often does not work when it comes to analytics. One precondition for extracting the most valuable insights possible using AI is to create the right algorithms. Propriety algorithms can be used to test competing models, and an advanced test can be used in conjunction with control analytics to isolate incremental impact. Data analytics can help establish rapid field experiments to test cause-and-effect relationships between certain strategic actions and the resulting key performance indicators, while highlighting opportunities to refine approaches to achieve maximum value. This minimizes risks across the portfolio of business investments. In today's health-care market, speed increasingly matters, so a delay of months, weeks, or even days in requested data analysis can be harmful clinically and competitively. There is often not the luxury of waiting.

Historically, the pharmaceutical industry and its executives have not been particularly quantitative, but they are now reacting to how the data revolution affects the competitive landscape and organizational context. Big data is not simply an IT problem, so it requires effective high-level management. When pursuing big data efforts, it is important to start with clear business objectives and not be overly ambitious. As part of this pragmatic process, in the beginning at least, smaller, specific business goals are better than broader, expansive goals. Leveraging data requires a change in management mindset and overcoming potential cultural barriers within the organization. The fundamental goal is to create a data-driven and evidence-based culture. Data collection and analytics should be embedded in the end user's work and the organizational culture, so the interface is as seamless as possible.

Data discovery is the first step on the pathway from vision to value, but there are some points of caution that pharmaceutical executives need to keep in mind. First, investing in big data technologies does not guarantee successful results. Second, a lack of senior management understanding or substandard communication can sometimes sidetrack a data analytics initiative. Third, sometimes data may surface an issue that management does not want to acknowledge. Fourth, health-care data needs to be put into the proper clinical context so incorrect conclusions are not drawn. Fifth, executives need to have sufficient insight to ask the right questions regarding the data. As it addresses these areas of concern, the pharmaceutical industry is indeed moving toward analytic decision-making with the goal of developing accurate, focused decisions.

Chapter 10

Data Analytics

Payers

PAYERS AND DATA ANALYTICS

In this chapter, we focus on the utility of data analytics for payers, principally insurance companies. From a financial standpoint, payers are the most consequential actor in the health-care ecosystem because they pay the bills. Payers face continual pressure to drive down costs while ensuring they receive value, particularly in terms of successful patient outcomes. In regard to data analytics, key questions for payers include how to enhance care coordination, how to create a more patient-centric health-care system, how to embrace new value-based payment models, how to incentivize preventive care by patients and providers, and how to be more collaborative across industry and organizational boundaries. Big data, the Internet of Things (IoT), and new technologies are driving the current revolution in the payer sector. Payers have practically limitless possibilities to improve processes, products, and services using big data. Unless they maintain currency with the latest trends, companies risk losing market share and experiencing lower profit margins. Data has always been crucial to the insurance industry and a key pivot point, particularly in terms of predicting outcomes and setting premiums. However, big data and accompanying technologies are taking that to another level. Across the health-care landscape, expenses are rising and margins are shrinking, so the major components of the health-care sector—principally patients, providers, and payers—are seeking data analytics to help address these challenges.

Data is an essential driver and enabler for insurance companies in moving rapidly to change their business models. Why is data now much more important? There are several drivers, but key factors include increases in the sheer volume of data, advances in complex statistical modeling techniques, and increased access to clustered parallel computing power. Two decades ago, models generally had to be built deductively based on formal hypotheses. Today, the combined power of data, statistics, and computing allows for a much more inductive approach (i.e., several variables can be thrown into a model to see what works and yield a workable model).

FOOTING THE BILL IN A CHANGING ENVIRONMENT

Insurance has historically been a slowly evolving business, but that pace has accelerated with changes in the broader health-care ecosystem. Payers are under continual pressure to quickly process and pay claims from a variety of sources (e.g., patients, clinicians, hospitals, and pharmacies). Most reimbursements are straightforward and valid, but some are complex and suspicious. Fraud, waste, and abuse are significant problems. The continued increase in medical expenses, along with the aging US workforce, fuels interest in data analytics efforts regarding loss prevention. Fraudulent claims ultimately translate into increased premiums for all policyholders. Some claims are unintentionally erroneous, and some are the result of gross fraud. Data analytics and automated alerts can discover fraudulent patterns that might evade a human responsible for reviewing claims manually.

At the same time, payers increasingly influence provider revenue cycle decisions. Reimbursement is tied to cost, quality, and outcomes data. Payers require providers to measure and report an increasing variety of quality metrics, including patient experiences, structures, processes, and outcomes. Payers are requiring providers to thoroughly understand their cost of providing services and to support reimbursement requests with data. The current environment demands that the right services are offered at the right facility with the correct level of quality and affordability. Providers can be tracked against clinical benchmarks and baseline operational metrics, and payers can encourage employers to implement wellness programs as part of risk management.

All components of the payer ecosystem are using analytics, including insurers, brokers, medical management companies, worker compensation services, and third-party administrators. Payers are engaged in an arms race to provide data analytics, and all of the major institutional actors are leveraging technology. As providers become more experienced with value-based reimbursement and accepting risk, they become a competitive threat. More and more providers are starting their own health insurance plans, which can allow them to boost their overall margins. This will further increase competitive pressures on payers.

PATIENT AS CONSUMER

Health insurance is less of a consumer-driven market than other components of the insurance sector (e.g., auto and home). For payers, data can be leveraged to help guide plan selection and customer enrollment. Big data can help insurance companies with their marketing, helping provide a more complete perspective on and view of customers. There is now greater personalization of health insurance products, which can be customized to provide consumers with more options, which is similar to retail-oriented industries. Sentiment analysis involves algorithms sifting through huge volumes of unstructured data, frequently either formal customer feedback (e.g., patient complaint or compliment email to a hospital) or informal social media activity (e.g., Facebook post), to create tailored marketing strategies for every customer. Sentiment-driven analytics can help payers develop personalized marketing of products and services. Consumers are generally willing to allow their data to be shared if there is a benefit (e.g., lower premiums) provided in return.

Analytics software can be used to provide highly tailored customer service for each policyholder. This can lead to increased customer satisfaction, greater word-of-mouth, and stronger loyalty. Big data can provide significant insights into customer actions, behavior, and preferences. New insurance products and services can be created based on these consumer preferences, including creating more targeted marketing campaigns. For example, analytics can be used to identify and proactively reach out to customers most at risk of cancelling their policies. Based on previous data, frequent calls to the help line may be a good predictor of whether someone is likely to leave.

Ultimately, to be fully meaningful, HCOs must be able to assess the root causes driving a deterioration or improvement in a member's overall health and wellness. Wearable technology can track fitness and health. Because the verification data exists, customers can be provided with incentives to lead healthier lifestyles. Activity trackers allow for monitoring a person's lifestyle habits (e.g., amount of exercise). Insurance companies are beginning to offer discounts to customers who agree to use a wearable monitor. Customers who consistently engage in a healthy lifestyle can achieve reduced premiums. Some ethical issues do arise. Now that the human genome is mapped and genetic profiling increasingly possible, insurance premiums could be set based at least in part on genetic makeup. This becomes an ethical issue because customers would be penalized based on factors they have no control over.

One challenge is to push analytics back down to the point of care. Providers are generating precisely segmented patient models based on a rich variety of variables. Payers and providers can use machine learning and predictive analytics to proactively engage those patients at greatest risk of readmission. The outreach includes care management, nursing attention, and specialist visits.

Insurance companies are increasingly more than a simple intermediary (i.e., just collecting premiums and paying claims). They are now expected to add value to the health-care equation in terms of improving health and wellness. Providers and payers are under pressure to reduce readmissions for several key indications: chronic obstructive pulmonary disease, congestive heart failure, pneumonia, total hip replacements, total knee replacements, and heart attacks. Increasingly, payers have to think like providers and encourage policyholders to make healthy decisions, so large payers are developing apps for the specific conditions and tailored cohorts of members. Similar to providers, payers are facing pressures to slow growth in health costs and increase patient wellness. When member health improves, there tend to be fewer adverse events (e.g., ER visits, hospital emergencies), which translates into lower medical costs. Payers can leverage their large, unique data sets to improve quality, access, and affordability, and they are also increasingly partnering with pharmaceutical companies to address health and wellness, particularly for chronic diseases such as diabetes and hypertension. For example, most prediabetics are unware that they have the condition; analytics can be used to identify and alert these individuals, preventing disease onset and lowering overall medical expenses. Medication adherence is another area where payers, providers, and pharmaceuticals can pursue meaningful, jointly beneficial collaboration.

SOURCES OF DATA FOR PAYERS

There is a transition to evidence-based medicine and value-based payments. Evidence-based medicine requires utilization of significant quantities of clinical data and current research, and value-based payments require increased sophistication in medical reporting, claims processing, process automation, and data management. Our ability to record, store, and analyze data has increased substantially in recent years. Combinations of data (e.g., claims, pathology results, and customer questionnaires) can be integrated to increase the accuracy and power of fraud detection. Data convergence refers to the capability to meaningfully integrate large quantities of data, both structured and unstructured, from a multitude of sources. There should be seamless extraction and integration of data.

There is a continual expansion of the sources of new data, including sensors, videos, and web chat logs; this includes an explosion in the volume and detail of patient data. IoT includes blood pressure and electrocardiogram monitors.

There are now adhesive bandages with biosensors capable of detecting early stages of sepsis. Open data initiatives by the US government and other entities have dramatically increased the quantity of available external data. This pooling of multiple external data sources increases the quantity and quality of insights that can be generated. Social media can be an especially rich source of data, much of it available in real time. Other sources of data include care management notes, claims, demographic and psychographic information, drug prescriptions, EHRs, lab results, medical images, and member surveys. Sources of data that can be used to cross-check and provide independent verification of diagnoses and procedures include EHRs, death records, driver licenses, and residency records; these can be automatically matched against claims. Most of the health-care data created today is unstructured, coming from sources such as clinical notes, digital devices, emails, imaging, laboratory tests, telematics, third-party sources, and video. In the insurance context, unstructured data includes hand-written notes from adjusters.

USES OF DATA BY PAYERS

Data analytics is a positive disruption for the insurance industry. Substantial benefits can accrue to those firms that dig deeper into their data. The goal is to convert payer data to information and then to actionable knowledge and ultimately to wisdom/insight for insurers. Payers can leverage data to create more efficient processes, drive productivity increases, and improve health outcomes. Big data facilitates application of behavioral analytics on huge sample sizes, with the potential to seamlessly manage the full life cycle of the claim. Data can help build more accurate profiles of health patterns. Insurance companies are continuing their ability to wring value out of data. In sum, the key sequential steps are to gain (1) data, (2) information, (3) knowledge, and (4) wisdom. Traversing the pathway from data to wisdom ultimately leads to better decision-making. In order to get there, payers need to leverage analytics, AI, and business intelligence.

Claims data can provide cost-reduction benefits. Big data can be used to predict which potential policyholders have a lower probability of filing a claim, and those individuals can be targeted as potential customers. Data analytics can be used to help payers evaluate claims variables (e.g., injury types by employee age or tenure, accident frequency by location or shift, and medical treatment utilized) that are the specific cost drivers for a given employee population. They can then take action to mitigate the causal issues. Data can provide a valuable window into workers' compensation programs, which can allow risk managers to pursue specific loss prevention actions, and payers can analyze post-loss data to help guide pre-loss safety initiatives. Analytics can be used to detect duplicate claims, medically unnecessary treatments, and providers who administer far above average numbers of procedures and tests. Eventually, with regard to fraud, payers can move from reaction and recovery to prediction and prevention, while still promptly paying valid claims. In brief, analytics can be used to predict, prevent, and recover losses from improper claims.

The uses of data include billing services, care management, claims adjustment, claims processing, Medicare/Medicaid program management, member services, overpayment detection, pharmacy benefit management, plan administration, performance optimization, provider data configuration, quality of care, regulatory compliance, revenue optimization, risk adjustment, and value-based insurance design. Ultimately, big data can produce longer, healthier lives for policyholders. Analytics can help improve the "Triple Aim" of health care introduced in Chapter 2 by enhancing the care experience, improving population health, and reducing costs.

As insurance becomes more and more of a commodity, analytics can be a source of competitive differentiation and can deliver a strong return on investment via a number of cost savings. Analytics can provide a more accurate forecast regarding the size and duration of claims based on comparing a new claim with similar ones in the past. This allows for better forecast on loss reserves, particularly for long-tail claims featuring chronic, degenerative health conditions. The company can then minimize the amount of money it has on hand, freeing that capital for other uses. Analytics can be used to assign more complex cases to more experienced adjusters. Insurance companies can score, prioritize, and allocate claims to a particular adjuster based on a match between the person's experience/expertise and the claim's characteristics. Analytics can help provide guidance on the propensity that a given claim will result in litigation. Those with a higher probability to result in defense of dispute claims can be assigned to more senior adjusters, who are more versed at settling claims earlier and for less amounts. This will help improve the company's loss adjustment expense ratio.

Risk scoring is a technique that insurance companies use to grade the health of each covered life. Risk scoring can be leveraged for health improvement and illness prevention. By using advanced analytics and big data technologies, disease-specific risk scoring can be particularly helpful in decreasing hospital admission and readmission, resulting in better overall health and lower total medical expenses. Risk scoring can be a competitive differentiator, but in order to have full impact, it must be comprehensive and predictive rather than partial (i.e., the data helps determine the aggregate distribution of risk adjusted payments but is not based on an individual member's holistic medical needs) or reactive (i.e., the data helps with risk adjustments going forward but does not help prevent medical difficulties).

As another valuable use of payer analytics, there is often an opportunity for subrogation. Text searches and semantic analysis of adjuster notes, medical records, police records, and other databases can identify subrogation opportunities. For example, the automated review of this data may find phrases and terms that are usually associated with a subro case. If successful, subrogation can generate increased loss recovery and decreased loss expenses. Analytics can also promote a more efficient settlement process, including creation of a fast-track claims settlement process. Data analytics can help optimize the limits in instant payouts and shorten claims cycle times. This promotes fairness, increased customer satisfaction, and reduced labor costs—eliminating instances of rushed, overpaying in claims settlement.

THINKING OUTSIDE THE BOX: PAYERS

Plamen Petrov, Director, Cognitive Technology, KPMG

Delivering high-quality services at an affordable cost is mission critical for health-care professionals and organizations. This is a formidable task in the knowledge and data intensive discipline of health care, where vast amounts of patient data and scientific and practitioner's knowledge are produced daily. Humans are just not capable by nature of ingesting, processing, understanding, and applying so much information. Luckily, advances in analytics and artificial intelligence (AI) come to the rescue. Mature analytics methods help payers organize and rationalize large volumes of data; advanced predictive analytics discover patterns and surface trends and correlations; and cutting-edge machine learning and AI technologies help payers interpret data, reason on facts, and learn from previous decisions and actions. Much like radiology and endoscopic surgery did years ago, AI and data science augment the expertise and capabilities of health-care professionals. By speeding up decision-making, reducing errors, and making knowledge and data available at the right time for payers, analytics is bringing health care to a whole new level, and driving down costs at the same time.

PAYER ANALYTICAL TOOLS

Traditional relational database technology is not equipped to handle the current variety and volume of unstructured data. Predictive analytics allows for comparison of millions of patient records by key factors such as age, gender, and ethnicity. Predictive analytics can highlight emerging risks and trends. AI and machine learning have been around for several decades. In recent years, these tools have become central to predictive analytics. Advanced analytical algorithms, including tools such as outlier analysis and predictive modeling, can be utilized to help identify improper claims. Machine learning involves technology engaging in self-learning, and it can help automate the decision-making process. Over time, the machine/system can learn to maximize true positives/negatives and minimize false positives/negatives, and it will become integrated with cognitive analytics via specialized software and the dynamic power of cloud computing. In the past, insurance companies often relied heavily on the experience or "gut feeling" of the adjuster to make important decisions. However, adjusters do not have time to manually sift through all the available information on all the claims. While that human factor remains, of course, it is now infused with data analytics.

Analytic algorithms can be used to analyze a multitude of billing patterns. Rule-based models can flag claim aberrancies, and relational network models can be used to detect improper activity because fraudulent billers frequently are connected with each other. Complex analytics software now allows for automatic detection of data anomalies. In particular, whereas the previous processes were managed manually, today automation is allowing for more frequent and more rapid decision-making. Algorithms can be used to reveal abnormal interactions between laboratories and providers, impossible or improper combinations of codes and procedures, claims that should be rejected or audited, excessive provider services for a given day, physician shopping, and outliers meriting additional investigation.

Machine learning algorithms can identify anomalies and patterns using massive quantities of unstructured historical claims data. Sometimes these outliers have benign explanations, but other times they are signs of fraudulent activity. Today, most fraud detection systems are rules-based. However, sophisticated perpetrators often know the rules and how to work around them to avoid detection. Predictive analysis makes it much more difficult to avoid detection because it uses a complex combination of rules, modeling, database mining, text scanning, AI, and machine learning to identify fraud earlier and more effectively during each step of the claims cycle.

Sophisticated statistical modeling allows us to develop a forecast of the future by comprehensively examining data from what happened in the past. Future applications will need to be agile and flexible in order to fulfill the needs of data scientists, business analysts, clinicians, executives, and other key stakeholders. Stream processing refers to the capability to immediately access, process, and analyze data in real time, which allows for rapid decision-making. Aggregation and querying happens now rather than later, potentially anticipating and preventing mortalities and other negative outcomes in the process. Many of the big data analytics tools work well with traditional office software, lessening the difficulty of accessing and utilizing large quantities of data. Hadoop is a big data processing application for Apache, and it is compatible with Excel, which allows for importation of data into formats insurance professionals are well acquainted with. Next generation applications need to be agile to meet the demands of developers, data scientists, business analysts, and executives so that the health-care industry can deliver improved patient outcomes at a lower cost. Rule-based automation, machine learning, and predictive analytics increase the accuracy and scalability of business operations, while reducing operating costs and, most importantly, benefiting patients.

PREMIUMS, RISK, AND STRATIFICATION

Premiums are the financial building blocks for insurance companies. Payers must set risk adjusted premiums high enough to cover costs and make a profit but low enough to attract and retain customers. Big data has fundamentally altered the equation to allow companies to implement smarter underwriting. For example, premium discounts can be offered for more active policyholders. The key is to offer customers a marketplace competitive yet still profit-making premium. Risk assessment is essential to this balancing act.

As an integral dimension to setting proper premiums, the core competency of the insurance industry is understanding and managing risk. By definition and by practice, the insurance industry is averse to risk. Both insurance companies and prospective policyholders take actions (e.g., amount of monthly premium, level of deductible) based on the anticipated level of risk. Payers are subject to risk hazards that can cause loss of revenue optimization. Big data offers a more accurate way to assess risk. Risk adjustment for purposes of internal operations and for government reimbursement requires complex data collection processes. The more information available the more understandable the risks and the better they can be managed. Insurance companies can no longer rely on static or slow to change actuarial tables to calculate risk. Insurers are tapping into monitors and sensors to better assess risk. One key goal is to identify high-risk patients and then manage their care to keep them out of ERs and hospital beds. Patient populations are increasingly stratified by condition, outcomes, risk, and utilization. Regulatory noncompliance is another source of risk. Payers typically need to submit member enrollment and claims data to government agencies such as the US Department of Health and Human Services. Data can help reduce the risk of fines, penalties, and non-reimbursement for noncompliance.

THE FUTURE: GREATER COLLABORATION AND CARE COORDINATION

Patients are receiving increasing varieties of care (e.g., medical devices, pharmaceuticals, social services) from a diverse range of providers (e.g., behavioral health facilities, hospitals, urgent care clinics). Thus, there is a sizable need for care coordination, which often requires greater integration of hospitals, specialists, and other providers; community resources (e.g., social workers); and payers. Improper post-discharge management is a leading cause of readmissions. Data can help facilitate care coordination, but there needs to be improved nationwide interoperability, which requires collaboration. The center of action between payers and providers used to be negotiations over rates. Payers and providers negotiate complex risk-based and value-based contracts. This requires drilling down into data across the entire continuum of care delivery, including detailed examination of claims information. While negotiating contracts remains important, there is now a greater focus on collaboration between health plans and hospital systems. Payers and providers are beginning to increase joint activities. Working together, many payers and providers are reimagining care delivery. Care coordination is a key element in alternative payment models and bundled payments. Increased cooperation between health data exchanges and HCOs is laying the foundation for eventual national interoperability across networks, which will stimulate care coordination and real-time data exchange. Platforms for interorganizational sharing of real-time data can lead to actionable alerts that improve care coordination.

Part III

BEST PRACTICES IN DATA ANALYTICS

Chapter 11

Data Quality

Meaningful and Systematic Use

FEATURES OF DATA QUALITY

HCOs manage substantial amounts of data that represent fundamental value for decision-making. Across the 6 Ps, effective data-based decision-making is predicated on the quality of the data being analyzed. Data quality is the usefulness of data to test, assess, or solve a particular problem for a given purpose. Acceptable data quality is crucial to operational and patient-level processes and to the trustworthiness of business analytics/business intelligence reporting. The quality of data has many features, which include the following:

- *Accuracy*. What is the correctness or validity of the data? Does the data represent the variables we intend to assess/measure?
- *Completeness*. Are all data provided? If not, what is missing?
- *Reliability*. Are the data consistent across data sources?
- *Relevance*. Are the data relevant for the problem being solved?
- *Accessibility*. Are all data accessible and up-to-date? If not, what are the restrictions?
- *Nature*. How are data distributed? What is the scale of measurement of the data?

The quality of the data should always be considered. It is best practice to take appropriate steps to routinely review and evaluate data. Data quality assurance is the process of verifying the utility of data by identifying inconsistencies and anomalies in data, then filtering the data to improve data quality. In this process, data are evaluated to identify incomplete, corrupt, or inaccurate parts of the data, and then to replace, correct, modify, or delete the biased data, if any are identified.

So much of what makes data "high quality" can really be managed from the start when data are first collected, recorded, and handled. A data quality assurance process can be routine and simple when data are appropriately handled and managed upfront, prior to any level of analytics.

HANDLING DATA TO MANAGE DATA QUALITY

Handling and managing data is an important step, as is anticipating the type of problems to be solved and how to most effectively utilize data to solve those problems. As the examples that follow illustrate, handling and managing health-care data can be quite challenging for a variety of reasons:

- *Source constraints.* Data may be stored in many different sources. A lack of interconnectedness between sources (e.g., EHRs, operations, HR, supply) can limit the ability for HCOs to effectively evaluate their data.
- *Capacity and time constraints.* Large amounts of data may need to be stored. The health-care industry acquires enormous quantities of data, from billing to patient care data. Filtering through so much data requires expertise and considerable time that often leads to backlogged requests across an organization.
- *Stability constraints.* Data can be highly volatile. While data may be readily available, there may not be a consensus on how the metrics are defined (e.g., length of stay at a hospital defined on a daily 24-hour scale vs. an hourly scale). This can result in discrepancies for performing analytics, making it difficult for analysts to effective utilize that data across metrics.
- *Accessibility constraints.* Data can be missing (e.g., due to a data entry error) or unknown (e.g., incomplete patient information). This can make analysis more challenging, especially as it relates to making actionable decisions.

Data quality is affected in many ways at each stage in which data are handled, from data entry to the storage, management, and retrieval of data. Figure 11.1 shows four stages where data are handled, and how data quality can be affected at each stage. In the next few sections we will elaborate on each stage, as it relates to data quality.

Data Entry

Data quality screening upfront, at the time data are acquired and entered as records, is key to managing the integrity of data quality throughout the data life cycle. It has become increasingly apparent that failing to utilize data quality procedures to identify and "cleanse" poor-quality data, even at this stage, may result in detrimental effects, from loss of market share to misdiagnosis of patients. An information system is a product of the data that are entered into it, which should be as accurate and reliable as possible. Nothing can threaten the trustworthiness of an information system used to create data reports faster than poor-quality data inputs. Data defects can result from a combination of issues, such as

- poorly structured domain definitions,
- substandard data entry training,
- defective program logic,
- flawed data verification and correction processes,
- inadequate time for data entry, and
- lack of incentives for quality data entry.

The best way to prevent these types of data quality issues from occurring in the first place is to standardize the data entry, such as by creating a data entry manual. Open communication with data entry personnel about the value and utility of the data being entered can be equally important. Certainly, data entry can be boring and often time-consuming. This can result in barriers for proper data entry, such as a lack of attention to the data entry task, and even efforts to cut corners to get data entry done quicker. Having checks and balances in the data entry stage can be instrumental to ensure high-quality data entry. Some steps that can be taken include the following:

- *Check data as it is collected.* Try to catch mistakes in data before it is entered into a database. Often data itself can be erroneous when it is entered. In these cases, while the data may technically be entered correctly, the data itself are incorrect.
- *Implement a data entry training protocol.* Establishing a training protocol can reinforce the value and importance of accurate data entry procedures. Take the time to let data enterers know what the data are used for so that they can see firsthand the value that is generated from the data that they enter.
- *Add incentives for accuracy.* Possibly, create a bonus structure to reward high-performing data enterers, create contests, and even generate data quality reports as part of an evaluation process to motivate a conscientious data entry process.
- *Formalize a data entry protocol.* As data are entered, have checks in place to catch mistakes. For example, have a master list of codes that data enterers can check as a resource in real time. If a code is entered incorrectly or not on the master list, this can be caught immediately.

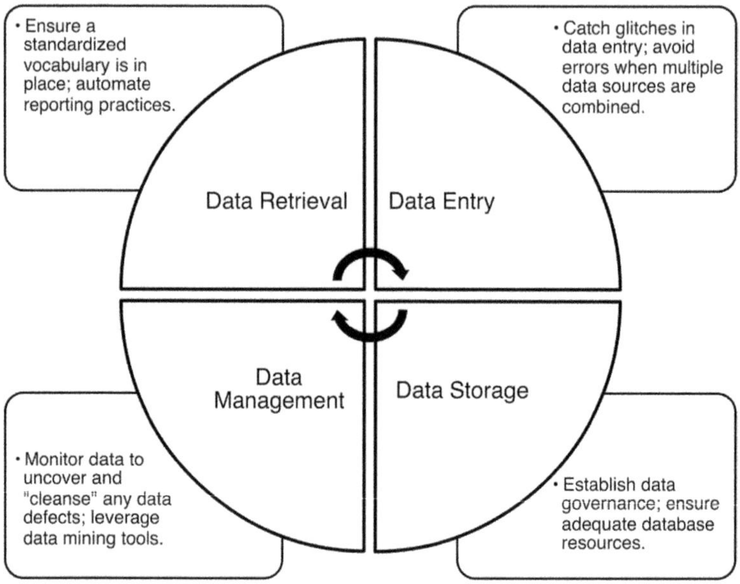

Figure 11.1 Four Stages of Data Handling in Health Care.

The database where data are entered and stored can also be checked to reveal data defects. Data profiling procedures can be used to (1) check for biased or "dirty" data, (2) "clean" the data by removing inconsistent and duplicate data, and then (3) reorganize existing data to ensure and verify the utility of a database for generating reports. Profiling data can be done manually or it can be automated with data quality tools that comply with HIPAA and the Federal Information Security Management Act (FISMA).

Data Storage

The capacity of an HCO to adequately archive or store data for use by a computer or device is vital. Different types can take many forms, from hard data storage to remote data storage, such as cloud computing, which has the potential to revolutionize how data is stored and accessed by users. Organizations need data managers just as much as they need managers for employees.

Data governance should be established at an *enterprise level*, meaning that the oversight for data should "prioritize the needs of an organization over individual users per se." Establishing a culture of data governance begins with administrative oversight of how, why, and where data are stored and accessed. Key features of data storage that must be managed or governed include the following:

- *The language and rules for data storage.* Data administrators are responsible for data modeling, establishing and maintaining the standardized vocabulary, and overseeing metadata. Metadata is used to summarize or describe information about data, such as data names and definitions, business rules, domains, data type, length, owner, and even file size. It is easier to track and work with specific data when there is adequate oversight of data storage and access that is facilitated by a common language for data to encourage the use and reuse of data.
- *The quality of data for decision-making.* Data quality stewards should be charged with preventing the storage of poor-quality data across an organization to ensure that stored data are high quality and thus can be readily utilized for decision-making at an enterprise level. HCOs should perform regular data audits on data storage and management systems to identify and resolve data quality issues. This process of reconciling data should be integrated into a continuous data quality improvement cycle.

Whether it contains claims data, financial records, EHR data, imaging dashboards, or diagnostic reports, a database repository should be as adaptable as possible. Data should be indexed and cataloged with clear data definitions and data source information to make it easier to manage the database and quicker to execute steps for data retrieval. Training is also important to ensure that data are standardized, handled, and stored properly using best practices. Human error is to be expected, even when HCOs have the appropriate data handling and storage protocols in place. Thus, critical thinking and vigilance at the data storage stage is crucial to effectively anticipate and correct problems with data.

Data Management

Data management is an essential part of effectively managing the information and data life cycle across an HCO. At an enterprise level, a database management system is used to provide an interface between the database where data are stored and the *end user* (i.e., the person who actually uses the data) to ensure that data are consistently organized and easily accessible. To ensure data security and data integrity, database management systems manage three important elements:

- the data that are stored
- the database where data are stored, modified, and accessed
- the standardized vocabulary or logical structure of the database

Data management provides centralized processes to manage data for consistent access by multiple users, from multiple locations. Central storage and management of data provides

- enhanced data security,
- reliable recovery from crashes and errors,
- robust data integrity and data trustworthiness,
- routine data logging and auditing capabilities,
- streamlined data abstraction and administration processes, and
- data locking for multiple users accessing a database concurrently.

Data management is part of the "checks and balances" needed to ensure that a database is trustworthy in terms of containing valid and reliable data for use by decision-makers across the 6 Ps. Managing data over the life cycle of the information stored requires data management procedures that are consistently applied and adaptive to the changing landscape of health care.

Data Retrieval

Retrieving or obtaining data, often from a database management system, is a key stage in analysis and decision-making. The steps to retrieve data should be structured and unambiguous in that the user should present a set of clear, unambiguous criteria in a query that allows for a data search based on the nomenclature or standardized vocabulary used to store the data. Data retrieval requires knowing where the data resides (e.g., such as in an EHR), and what the specified data attributes entail (e.g., data definitions, value sets, business/clinical coded content).

Data retrieval is an increasingly complex task, especially as health care shifts to a big data model with huge volumes of EHR and as other new applications allow for the entry, storage, and management of huge volumes of data across the 6 Ps. It is increasingly important to manage the retrieval process in a way that leads to the extraction of the all data requested for assessment/analysis. Key factors for safeguarding an efficient retrieval process include

- identifying and tracking all data sources,
- migrating and integrating data across divergent sources,
- ensuring that only authorized users make requests,
- specifying inclusion/exclusion criteria for a data request,
- entering fields of interest when making a data request, and
- integrating reviews and approvals to release information.

A big challenge for users, especially those who lack meaningful knowledge of what data are stored and how data are stored, is simply knowing what to ask for. It is crucial that data requests are aligned with the nomenclature or language of the database or other applications being searched. Often, it is recommended that users making a data request first coordinate with the health information management teams who are largely responsible for ensuring that data are accurate and complete. Alternatively, publishing a portal or other source that describes all the datasets available to users can help facilitate a more consistent, effortless data retrieval process.

THINKING OUTSIDE THE BOX: THE VALUE OF MANAGING DATA QUALITY

Steven Press, Operations Research Analyst, US Department of Homeland Security

The uncovering of hidden patterns, relationships, and insights would not be possible without having accurate, accessible, and complete data in an analytical environment. Having held key analytical and decision-making roles within many organizations, in several different industries, I have seen firsthand the value that business intelligence (BI) and data analytics provide. The decisions made within all of these organizations were based upon analytical evaluations derived from well-structured data and BI. Whether the decision involved analyzing financial data points and credit risk or required the evaluation of hundreds of potential products and their related factors to determine an upcoming product line, none of it would have been possible without data analytics. The flow of information is occurring faster and faster. Thus, being able to sift through the data and identify insights for immediate decisions is absolutely critical to stay ahead in competitive environments.

DATA RECOVERY

Recovering damaged or lost data is instrumental to ensure data quality. Not having a plan in place for recovering data can be detrimental to an HCO. Indeed, HIPAA and the Health Information Technology for Economic and Clinical Health Act (HITECH) require HCOs to develop valid data recovery plans for situations in which systems containing protected electronic health information are damaged.[1] The aim of these laws is to strengthen privacy

1 National Archives and Records Administration. (2013). Federal Register. Retrieved from https://www.federalregister.gov/documents/2013/01/25/2013-01073/modifications-to-the-hipaa-privacy-security-enforcement-and-breach-notification-rules-under-the.

and security protections for health information. They include regulations for HCOs at an enterprise level for the following areas:

- data backup
- data recovery protocols
- testing and improvement
- analysis of the criticality of data
- periodic testing of a data recovery plan

The key parts to a strong data recovery plan are (1) preparation and planning, (2) routine data backup, and (3) routine testing of the data recovery plan. For preparation and planning, risk analysis is key. Assessing financial loss or misdiagnosis risks that would occur if data were lost is imperative. It is really not a matter of "if" but a matter of "when" data recovery is needed. It is therefore critical to adequately plan and prepare for this imminent, real threat. Routine data backup can further safeguard HCOs against lost or damaged data.

Testing and analyzing data criticality is part of the "checks and balances" to ensure that data recovery plans are valid. As the climate of health care evolves, so should a data recovery plan. Testing and analyzing critical elements of the data life cycle, such as the capacity and comprehensiveness of data storage and whether data access protocols are sufficient, is critical. This step strengthens an HCO's confidence that critical data are stored and can be accessed as needed, often in real time.

SAFEGUARDING DATA INTEGRITY

There is an adage that "some data are better than no data." This is erroneous advice because "bad" data can lead to "bad" decisions, such as negative outcomes for HCOs and for patients. Safeguarding the integrity of data is therefore instrumental to ensuring that the data we have will lead to good decisions. Data integrity is the validity and trustworthiness of data over its life cycle. Safeguarding data integrity across the stages of data entry, storage, management, and retrieval facilitates valid and reliable analytics-driven decision-making.

Data integrity is vital for decision-making, both in terms of the data itself and the processes implemented to handle the data. In this way, data integrity can be thought of as a state and as a process:

- *Data integrity as a state*. As a state, we are referring to the data itself, specifically the data points and data sets. Data integrity as a state includes standardization of data according to data models/types, and data uniformity/completeness based on business rules and definitions. The related questions we may ask include the following: Is missing, omitted, incomplete, or inaccurate data evident in EHR records? Are EHR fields filled in consistently and in a timely manner? Are data appropriately entered into corresponding fields (e.g., numeric cells should only accept numeric, not alphabetic, data)?

- *Data integrity as a process.* As a process, we are referring to the processes for handling data and measures used to verify that data is trustworthy across the data handling life cycle. Data undergoes many operations to support decision-making, such as entry, storage, maintenance, retrieval, and recovery. In this way, data verification, correction, and data retrieval processes reflect data integrity strategies and contribute to the optimization of data utility and analytics-driven strategies for decision-making.

Efforts to ensure data integrity reflect data security initiatives, such as those used to safeguard against programming errors or malicious data breaches or hacks. Database security is therefore an extension of data integrity best practices, which include strategies that are part of data recovery plans, data encryption, locks, and controls to secure or protect data. Software and database developers can facilitate security efforts by defining integrity constraints to enforce business rules on data entry.

Developing systems to ensure high data quality is vital to the success of HCOs in utilizing data for analytics-driven decision-making. Maintaining data integrity is important to ensure valid and reliable processes that can

- synchronize data handling procedures,
- facilitate the search and recovery of data,
- enable the ability to trace the origin of stored data, and
- support the use and maintenance of data at an enterprise level.

Data integrity is essentially a proxy for data quality. Safeguarding the integrity of data is thereby essential for the effective utility of analytics-driven business processes and decision-making in health care.

DRIVING ANALYTICS TO AUGMENT DATA QUALITY

While the life cycle of data is critical in its entirety, the ultimate goal of data quality assurance practices is to facilitate effective utilization of data to drive quality decision-making. Therefore, best practices for data quality ensure that when data are accessed, they can be trusted for use in decision-making across the 6 Ps. The vital role that data plays in decision-making is what drives the need for strategic data quality plans and processes.

Once accessed, data takes on a life of its own, and analytics is the driving force by transforming data that are accessed into information that can optimize strategic decision-making for HCOs. The ability of analytics to drive decision-making is largely dependent on the quality and integrity of the data inputs.

The utility of analytics has less to do with having enough data, and more to do with having enough high-quality data. The central purpose of analytics in health care is to optimize decision-making across the 6 Ps. Best practices in data analytics extends beyond the use of analytics itself to include the overall decision-making process, which can be broadly summarized in six phases of problem-solving:

- *Recognize.* From HCOs to patients, we first recognize a problem to be solved, which can be identified across the healthscape taxonomy (see Figure 2.1 in Chapter 2). HCOs may address compliance or operations questions, whereas patients may focus more on their own health. Problems to be solved exist when there is a gap between what we know and what we need to know.
- *Operationalize.* The problem can often be complex, making it a vital step to define the problem. The complexity of the problem largely lies in the symptoms to be addressed. For example, long ER waiting times for patients might stem from improper staffing (e.g., not enough staff), insufficient facilities (e.g., too few ER rooms), or external factors (e.g., random peak visit times). The problem may be defined as improving patient satisfaction, redesigning ER facilities, or optimally hedging peak visit times.
- *Structure.* This is the key phase to set the stage for analysis. In this phase, we plan for analysis, state goals and objectives, choose appropriate analytics for analysis (descriptive, predictive, or prescriptive; see Figure 3.1 in Chapter 3), and identify or anticipate constraints or restrictions (e.g., budgetary limitations to implement solutions). For example, for the ER problem we can renovate or even relocate the ER (where?), change protocols for how patients are received and processed when in the ER (how?), and change the amount of staffing (how much?).
- *Analyze.* Once the problem is structured for analytics, we implement the analysis and interpret outcomes. This is a key phase where data analytics plays the largest role in terms of impacting decision models and processing and analyzing data for decision-making. At this stage, we convert data into information, which can be used to inform decision-makers about a problem to be solved. Information results from processing, organizing, structuring, or presenting data in a meaningful or useful manner. Accessing

high-quality data for analysis is truly essential in this stage to ensure that data analysis outputs lead to trustworthy decisions in the next stage.

- *Decide*. Making decisions is always risky. All models include some degree of risk in health-care settings. However, while analytics cannot capture all details in all settings, to the extent that data inputs can be trusted, analytics can drive optimal decision-making across the 6 Ps. For example, to identify what renovations to make to an ER, we may use analytics to prioritize which renovations to make; however, given constraints or limitations (e.g., facility costs), some high priority renovations may never be completed or may be completed in different ways than initially intended.
- *Act*. The true test of an analytics model is its usefulness for decision-making in the real world. Implementing a solution is the ultimate test of the utility of analytics for HCOs and patients. Being adaptive over time as a solution is implemented is important. Health care is not static. It is dynamic. Thus, so too should be the use of analytics to solve problems in the health-care ecosystem.

The quality of decision-making is dependent on the integrity of the data being used. Communication from analysts to managers, to executives, to patients is vital. The process of problem-solving reflects a transition from data to information that, with high-quality data, can optimize decision-making, but without it, can be misleading. In this way, data quality and the integrity of the data handled is an essential feature in all phases of the problem-solving process. Thus, the use of best practices for data quality assurance is a vital part of analytics utility across the 6 Ps.

REFERENCE

National Archives and Records Administration. (2013). Federal Register. Retrieved from https://www.federalregister.gov/documents/2013/01/25/2013-01073/modifications-to-the-hipaa-privacy-security-enforcement-and-breach-notification-rules-under-the.

Chapter 12

Exposition of Data

Managing Data Queries and Sampling

FUNDAMENTAL QUESTIONS ACROSS THE 6 Ps

Data are meaningful only inasmuch as they can inform decision makers. In analytics, asking the right questions is vital to success. Framing a business or clinical question properly is critical to ensure that an analysis leads to valid and reliable insights that drive optimal decision-making.

The questions asked by decision makers at each of the following stages of data handling and management are critical to ensure the collection and accessibility of meaningful data:

- Data collection to ensure that relevant data are collected and can be used later to answer fundamental questions and solve problems at an enterprise level.
- Data storage to ensure that language and rules for data storage are screened, and that high-quality, valid data are safeguarded.
- Data management to ensure that the interface between the database where data are stored and the *end user* (i.e., the person who uses the data) are reliably organized and easily accessible.
- Data retrieval to ensure that data are structured and unambiguous for a query or data search that allows access to relevant data, while also ensuring discretion for patient data.

Meaningful use of data has seen a shift toward queries that focus on care. Across the healthscape taxonomy (see Figure 2.1 in Chapter 2), business and clinical initiatives and queries are increasingly required to show a linkage to positive patient outcomes. Indeed, recall that we opened this book in Chapter 1 by identifying not only the industries that constitute the 6 Ps but also the key types of questions that are asked. Many areas of concern relate directly to positive patient outcomes across the 6 Ps, including the following:

- Enhanced quality of patient care, such as questions from *policy makers* related to incentivizing patients to be preventive, and from *payers* to incentivize more patient-centric health care.
- Increased access to care, such as questions from *providers* for how to engage in more effective population health management, and from *pharmaceuticals* for how to be more collaborative across industry and organizational boundaries.
- Reduced costs associated with care, such as questions from *pharmacies* to embrace new value-based payment models, and from *patients* for how to take on the role of money manager given increasingly high deductibles and coinsurance.

Fundamental questions across the 6 Ps are becoming increasingly patient-centric. HCOs are mindful of the need to drive the success of their organizations with considerate leadership and decision-making utilizing analytics to drive enhanced quality of, increased access to, and reduced costs of care to patients in and out of the health-care system. This is the true *value* of analytics—to utilize vast amounts of data that can optimize outcomes for HCOs via patient-centric, value-based decision-making.

THINKING OUTSIDE THE BOX: ASKING QUESTIONS THAT ARE LEVERS TO VALUE

Edwin K. Morris, President and Founder, Pioneer Knowledge Services

Seeing what is not there takes imagination, and that imagination is fueled by a never-ending intrinsic desire to ask *why* and *what if* questions; questions that can be readily answered using analytics. Seeking to answer these questions allows me to seek improvements to processes and situations, and to add clarity to the creative visualization process. Fostering a behavior of inquiry is a necessary element to improvement and growth. Allowing the culture to add value makes it participatory and reflective. My first recognition for this talent was in the US Army, many years ago. I asked important questions about processes, and I suggested an alternative that was applied and adaptive. For the value my questions led to, I was awarded my first Army Achievement Medal. I thought, how am I the first to ask these questions? Maybe I was not the first, but all organizational change is incremental. For this reason, I say, engage your seekers to have a voice—to ask questions that are levers to value.

CONCEPTUALIZING THE DATA LIFE CYCLE

As data are stored and managed for data query capabilities, and more and more data are retrieved for analysis, query processes must be modified and updated over time so that HCOs can gradually augment and fine-tune their database use. This is an essential part of a continuous learning model, where HCOs build business intelligence over time as data are stored, modified, and utilized across industries.

Making use of data likewise requires the realization of analytical tools across the data life cycle, from data exploration to decision-making and data optimization. For this reason, let us first take a closer look at the data life cycle across the health-care ecosystem. A summary of the value and usefulness of analytics across the data life cycle is given in Figure 12.1.

At an exploration stage, end users identify problems to be solved and evaluate and generate questions. Across the healthscape, this can relate to the business end (e.g., How to close the gap between costs of service and operating expenses?) and the clinical end (e.g., How to most effectively integrate patients as part of a caregiver team?) of the taxonomy. Considerations at this stage should be considerate of *value* as questions are generated and problems are identified to ensure a match between patient-centricity and mission focus. Questions to be generated and the problems identified can be

- reactive, typically as sudden changes occur (e.g., passage of new laws that require revisions to reporting mandates);
- routine, typically as part of mission-driven business-as-usual management (e.g., patients exercise and dieting routines, or HCO evaluation of employee performance and patient satisfaction reports); or
- proactive, typically as a means to drive innovation and be forward-thinking (e.g., developing new, less invasive treatment options for patient care, such as the Insulin Pen for routine Type 1 and Type 2 diabetes care).

At an investigation stage, end users make data queries based on analytics models built to assess the relevant data being requested. Matching data requests to ensure that data retrieval processes extract highly useful data is vitally important to optimal decision-making across the 6 Ps. Not having processes in place to ensure that queries lead to the retrieval of high-integrity data can lead to poor decision-making and misleading insights. Some important steps that should be taken to ensure continuous development and improvement of data query processes include the following:

- Identify data queries that are made most often by building indices that optimize the frequency of data query processes. Once a Structured Query

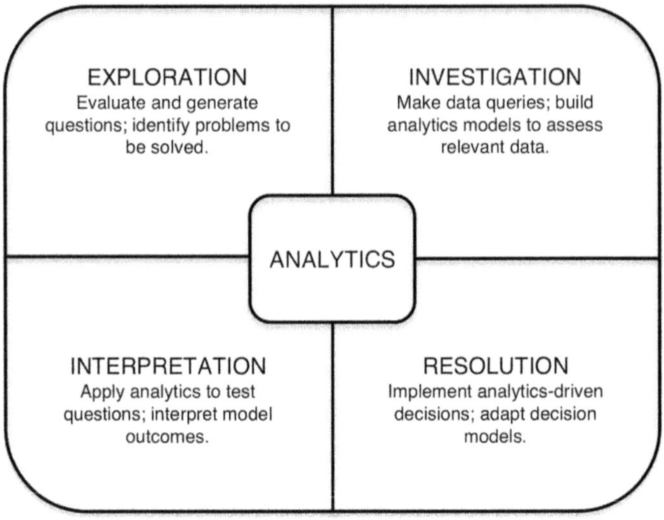

Figure 12.1 Utilizing Analytics Across the Data Life Cycle.

Language (SQL) is established, estimate the frequency of each SQL statement to prioritize queries that are made most often.

- Prioritize the most important queries. Importance is a relative term, relating to an organization and to an end user. To illustrate, requests for data routinely evaluated to identify profit margins by executives may be more important than requests by assistants for data that are not vitally related to the success of an organization.
- Avoid arbitrary limits on the number of indices that can be created for a database. Including limits or constraints on indices can impede data query searches. As a best practices guideline, create indexes as necessary to support database queries, and only limit the number of indices when doing so can help avoid inefficiencies related to data modification.

At an interpretation stage, analytical models are tested and outcomes are interpreted based on the questions being asked and problems identified. Developing appropriate analytics models requires industry insights and expertise. The data and the interpretations must match in terms of the informativeness of analytics. For example, if the aim for applying analytics is to evaluate the current position of an organization compared to peer organizations, then descriptive statistics ("What has happened?") are practical. However, if the aim is to predict changing trends in the marketplace to gain a competitive advantage over peer organizations, then predictive analytics ("What could happen?") or prescriptive analytics ("What should we do?")

are most practical to "match" the analytics with what is to be learned. Factors to be carefully considered when interpreting outcomes include the following:

- *The scale of measurement of the data queried.* Optimal decisions typically can be made from data in an interval or ratio scale of measurement.
- *The distribution of the data inputs.* Optimal decisions can typically be made from data that are normally distributed.
- *Whether the data added as inputs to a model are comprehensive.* Optimal models include all factors relevant for analysis.
- *Which analytics tools were chosen to answer questions and resolve problems.* Different analytics tools are optimal for answering different types of questions.
- *The likelihood of observing the outcomes reported in an analysis.* Models typically start with an assumption that the factors added to a model have no effect on the outcomes of interest; outcomes that are particularly important in a model tend to have less than a 5 percent likelihood of occurring, if this assumption were true.

At a resolution stage, analytical models lead to the implementation of decisions, often at an enterprise level, and considerations are made to allow decision processes to be adaptive as data and situational factors change. Not only should considerations be made for what to do, but also, there should be reflective considerations for how models should be adapted or changed. In other words, we can learn as much about how to redesign and adapt vital processes in the data life cycle to optimize analytics models as we can about decisions that are more organizational-specific based on the outputs from these models. There are several questions to consider at the decision and resolution stage:

- Are data inputs valid and reliable?
- Are the assumptions of the analytics models met?
- Are current environmental factors (e.g., economic or policy) accounted for?
- Are the decisions suggested by an analytics model feasible based on existing organizational or individual resources?
- How should decisions be prioritized in cases where an analytics model leads to many possible decision options?

In all, the data life cycle is an important part of the utility of analytics across the 6 Ps. Optimal decision-making is consequently dependent on the effective utility of data at each stage of the data life cycle.

SAMPLING TECHNIQUES

HCOs are interested most often in addressing population-level outcomes, such as outcomes related to the satisfaction levels of all patient experiences, or factors that have the greatest impact on profit margins enterprise-wide. However, obtaining population data can be difficult, if not unrealistic in many cases, such as obtaining satisfaction data from all patients who enter a hospital, or obtaining all data across an enterprise. For this reason, it is advantageous to develop sampling procedures to obtain sample data that are from a portion of an entire population, but that can still reliably yield results from which analysts can draw conclusions regarding an entire population.

Sampling is necessary because HCOs often do not have access to all data in a population. For this reason, analysts use data from samples (a portion of data from the population) to make inferences concerning a population. Sampling methods help analysts collect data that are representative of the larger population so that results observed in those samples can be generalized to those populations of interest.

If analysts want to generalize the results they observe in a sample to those in the larger population, then they need sampling methods that ensure that the sample is representative of the larger population. A representative sample is a sample that has characteristics that resemble those in the population. Characteristics of interest include demographic factors (e.g., race, gender, age, and place of birth), financials, health trends, medical needs, education, insurance status, and more.

When characteristics in a population are known, which can often be the case, sampling procedures can be used to ensure that population characteristics will also be represented or included in the sample that is selected from that population. Some common sampling techniques most often used in analytics to achieve the selection of representative samples include the following:

- *Simple Random Sampling.* This method of sampling utilizes a random procedure to ensure that sampling subsets of data or individuals from a population are entirely achieved at random, such that the data or individuals selected had an equal chance of being selected.
- *Systematic Sampling.* With this method of sampling, the first individual is selected using simple random sampling, and then every *n*th person is systematically selected until all participants have been selected.
- *Stratified Random Sampling.* With this method of sampling, a population is divided into subgroups or strata; data or individuals are then selected from each subgroup using simple random sampling and are combined into one overall sample.

- *Cluster Sampling.* With this method of sampling, subgroups or clusters of data or individuals are identified in a population, and then a portion of clusters that are representative of the population are selected such that all individuals in the selected clusters are included in the sample. All clusters that are not selected are omitted from the sample.

As noted earlier in this book, a key goal for data partitioning is to select samples or "sets" using a random procedure, which is called *probability sampling* (see Figure 3.2 in Chapter 3). One of the hallmarks of probability sampling is that it results in an unbiased "set" because the procedures ensure that data or individuals selected had an equal chance of being selected.

To ensure that the probability of selecting each data point or individual is the same, a *sampling with replacement* procedure is typically required. Using this type of procedure, each selection is replaced before the next selection is made. To illustrate, suppose we selected data from a small bank of 10 EHR records. The probability of selecting the first record is 1 in 10 or 10 percent. If we return the record we selected back into the bank before selecting again, then 10 records will remain in the bank when we select again, and the probability of the next selection will again be 1 in 10 or 10 percent. However, this is not how we typically select data for analysis.

Typical data sampling procedures do not replace data as data are selected. Instead, a *sampling without replacement* procedure is used where each selection is not replaced before the next selection is made. To illustrate, suppose we did not replace the first EHR record we selected from the data bank before selecting the second record. In this case, the probability of selecting the first record is still 10 percent. However, for our second selection, there would only be 9 records remaining in the bank, so the probability of the next selection will be 1 in 9 or 11 percent. Thus, each selection is not associated with the same likelihood of being selected using sampling without replacement.

The norm for data in health care, such as EHRs, is that the data populations are so large that even if analysts use sampling without replacement, the changes in probabilities from one selection to the next are largely negligible. For example, even with only 100 records, the probability of the first selection is 1 in 100 or 1 percent, and the probability of the second selection is 1 in 99, which is about 1 percent again. The difference in probability is negligible. With a database containing millions of records, which is typical in health care, it simply does not matter whether or not you replace data as it is selected; the change in likelihood of selecting data will be negligible. You can see that while each selection is not replaced before the next selection is made, the likelihood of each selection is still about the same. Thus, sampling without replacement can be used to select simple random samples from large populations of data.

While selecting data at random is important to select an unbiased data set for analysis, it does not always mean that the data set will necessarily be representative of the characteristics in a population. When data selection is left completely to chance, this can lead to the selection of a data set that is not representative of the population. For example, by chance, financial records could be overrepresented for a certain time period, or EHRs could be underrepresented for a given demographic (e.g., gender, race, age). When data selection is left entirely to chance, we can, by chance, select a sample that has dissimilar characteristics in proportion to the larger population of interest. There are two simple solutions to ensure that samples selected are proportionally representative of a population of interest:

- *Undersampling.* This sampling strategy adjusts down certain types of individuals or data, particularly for characteristics that are less represented in a population. For example, analysts sampling billing data for delinquent medical accounts may adjust down families from higher household income brackets given the lower likelihood that such families will have delinquent accounts.
- *Oversampling.* This sampling strategy adjusts up certain types of individuals or data, particularly for characteristics that are more represented in a population. For example, analysts sampling marketing data for breast cancer screenings may adjust up the proportion of women in the sample given the greater risks and thus greater need to market breast cancer screenings for women.

Effort to ensure a sample is representative of a population is sometimes called *quota sampling* or *proportional sampling*. No matter what it is called, the aim is to ensure that characteristics in a sample resemble those in the population from which analytics will be used to drive decision-making. Combined with random sampling procedures, these strategies ensure the selection of unbiased, representative samples that can be used for analysis to inform decision makers about what is happening in the larger population, and what can be done about it.

THE ACCURACY OF SAMPLING

Sampling is remarkably accurate in informing analysts about characteristics or trends in a population, and thus is a valuable tool for decision-making. While any sampling strategy is associated with some probability of error, we can measure this error and use it to gain insights into the likelihood that our decisions will yield desired outcomes. Two key features of selecting samples deserve particularly close consideration when utilizing sampling analytics:

- *Sampling error* is the extent to which sample statistics selected from the same population differ from one another. This difference, which occurs by chance, is measured by the standard error of the mean.[1] As a rule, the smaller the sampling error or standard error, the more accurate decisions that can be made using analytics tools.
- *Sampling bias* occurs when a sampling procedure employed favors certain data types or groups over others, resulting in a nonrepresentative sample. For this reason, it is important for a data query to specify inclusion and exclusion criteria to ensure that certain groups or data types are not over or underrepresented in the data that are retrieved.

Sampling bias can be readily resolved by ensuring proper, thoughtful sampling procedures during the data query and retrieval stages. Sampling error, however, will be important even for the most representative samples. A sample is only a portion of all data available, and thus there is some variability with samples in the accuracy of the decisions made about populations.

For issues of sampling, the key consideration is statistical power. Statistical power represents the likelihood that a data sample can detect an effect in a population, assuming the effect actually exists. For example, a pharmaceutical company may test the efficacy of a new drug treatment that they believe can reduce symptoms of schizophrenia. Statistical power represents the likelihood that they will be able to demonstrate this effect, if in fact they are correct and the effect of the drug indeed reduces symptoms of schizophrenia. Statistical power can range from 0 percent (i.e., zero likelihood of detecting the effect, if it exists) to a perfect 100 percent (i.e., certain likelihood of detecting the effect, if it exists).

As you can imagine, statistical power is quite important with sampling. The larger the statistical power, the more confident we can be that a sample will yield expected effects, if indeed those effects are real. As a general rule, statistical power is considered acceptable if it is at least 80 percent. For anything below that, it is hard to justify the use resources to conduct the sampling. The reason for this is sometimes referred to as the "needle in a haystack problem"—with low power, it can be difficult to "find" or detect an effect, even if it exists.

One straightforward way to increase power is to increase the size of the sample. This method of increasing power is based on the law of large numbers. The law of large numbers explains that the larger the sample size, the smaller the standard error, and thus the larger the power to detect effects in a population. The logic is quite simple. Imagine you sample from a population of 100 units. Do you trust a decision about that population based on data collected from a sample of 10 units or from a sample of 90 units? Well, 90, of course, because that sample had more information about the population.

---

1 Privitera, G. J. (2017). *Research Methods for the Behavioral Sciences* (2nd ed.). Thousand Oaks, CA: Sage Publications.

Likewise, the larger that a sample is, the more data or information that you have, and the better your decisions will be regarding the effects or trends in a population.

FEATURES OF SAMPLING AND DATA QUERIES

Sampling is typically used when it is not feasible to analyze all data in a given population. When population or enterprise-scale data are not accessible in one way or another, analysts select a relatively smaller, randomly selected subset of data from that larger population. Many analytics platforms use some sort of sampling to create and develop reports and analysis. When sampling is used, it is important to recognize that only some data are available to guide decision-making. It can be evident that sampling is used in cases when

- only a portion or segment of a population is queried, such as by demographics or by region, or
- sampling secondary dimensions in data that represent subsets within a larger data set or database.

Sometimes the need for sampling can result simply from the nature of what is queried. While sampling can be quite accurate, it can be advantageous to avoid sampling to avoid sampling error altogether. There are several strategies to avoid the need for sampling:

- *Limiting the search range.* If you can constrain your search to require a smaller range of data, such as across months or years, this can increase the likelihood that all data can be retrieved from the more limited search range.
- *Querying standardized, well-established reports.* Data that are well coded, such as financial reporting, can yield population data, whereas details in an EHR can be less consistent and more difficult to fully retrieve.
- *Reducing the complexity of data storage and retrieval processes.* The collection of data across multiple filters, sites, or databases can increase the complexity of retrieving data, thereby leading to subsets of data for analysis.
- *Utilizing big data.* The 6 Ps generate sets so large that a standard computer would not be able to open the data file. Analyzing big data eliminates the need for sampling by the sheer size of the data sets alone. Having a physical infrastructure in place to handle big data is vital.

SAMPLING AND THE BIG DATA SOLUTION

It was not too long ago that the idea of analyzing big data, all of it, was not even a point of consideration. The capabilities of handling all of that data, let alone analyzing it, was overwhelming. Sampling was thus a pragmatic necessity. Today, however, this is no longer the case. Computing power and neural networks can handle vast amounts of data and process it for analysis. What is distinctive about big data is the ability to apply advanced analytics tools (e.g., data mining) to analyze vast and diverse data sets.

Across the 6 Ps, it can be difficult to meaningfully process, analyze, and report all of the data stored, which makes sampling a pragmatic necessity. With big data, however, sampling is not needed. Yes, you must select the data you need and ensure that you have the correct or appropriate data for analysis. However, with big data capabilities, the possibilities for retrieving the right data are endless. This is especially true for rare or uncommon data that would be otherwise difficult to sample or find with a basic query search without implementing big data capabilities.

Big data has the potential to eliminate the need for sampling, at least for those industries that can build or bring in the necessary expertise and resources to establish a big data infrastructure. The capabilities of mining and data visualization tools operate with such large data sets that the limitations of sampling, such as sampling error, simply do not apply. Big data therefore offers vast statistical samples that complement analytics tools which are optimized for large data sets. Consistent with the law of large numbers, big data brings very large data samples that lead to more accurate statistics and thus, by extension, more accurate decision-making.

REFERENCE

Privitera, G. J. (2017). *Research Methods for the Behavioral Sciences* (2nd ed.). Thousand Oaks, CA: Sage Publications.

Chapter 13

Driving Actionable Data

Triggers, Indicators, and Statistical Inference

DRIVING ACTIONABLE DATA

Effectively evaluating projects, plans, and processes is becoming increasingly essential to organizational success, which includes fields of medicine and health care where change is a continuous feature across the 6 Ps ecosystem. Effectively utilizing analytics requires policies for routine implementation at an enterprise level. Analytics-driven health care is part of a culture shift aimed at driving effective decision-making across numerous sectors and industries and across the entire landscape of the 6 Ps ecosystem.

For analytics to be an effective tool, it needs to utilize actionable data, or data that is useful or that can be transformed into information that can be used for making effective decisions and drawing meaningful conclusions. *Information*, defined in Chapter 11, is the result of transforming data into a meaningful or useful array for the purpose of analysis and decision-making. In this way, analytics *informs* decision makers; data is the "fuel" that drives decision-making. For analytics to be effective, the data itself must be actionable, which means, at a minimum, the following standards are met:

- The data collected is high-integrity, high-quality data.
- Data standardization, maintenance, and cleaning tools ensure that data are entered and modified correctly across the data life cycle, and can be retrieved at an enterprise level.
- Data queries retrieve valid and reliable data that are relevant to the decisions that need to be made, and return complete data needed for analysis.
- Data collection for analysis is appropriate with the correct data organized for analysis to answer the correct, corresponding questions being asked by decision makers.

- Data analysis stages employ the correct, appropriate analytic tools for the types of data being analyzed.

Actionable data is often thought of as a buzzword, but it really has genuine meaning and application for the quality and effectiveness of decision-making with analytics. It goes back to the adage that "you get out what you put in." In other words, the more actionable the data we put in, the more we get out in terms of leveraging data for effective, optimal decision-making.

DISTINGUISHING ACTIONABLE DATA FROM NOISE

In contrast to actionable data is *noise,* which is data that is meaningless, redundant, corrupt, or even non-interpretable (e.g., unstructured text). In the context of noise, we typically refer to data that is actionable as the signal, which is a term used to describe data or information of interest from which actionable decisions can be made. The fundamental concern is that data, no matter how high in quality, indubitably contain some level of noise that we need to filter in order to detect the signals that will lead to effective, optimal decision-making.

Identification of signals in noisy data can be challenging because a potential signal depends critically on the extent to which a priori assumptions of the noise are correct in a model, and depends on whether we are using an appropriate analytics model to detect it, measure it, and even remove it.[1] The following are two key challenges associated with noisy data:

- *Concept drift* relates to the adage "the only constant is change." It is not unusual at all that the target "concept" we are trying to predict changes over time (e.g., employee turnover, profit margins, patient health behaviors). When such change is difficult to anticipate, this can create noise, and it can reduce the accuracy of our predictions over time.
- *Data contamination* relates to data integrity and refers to the malicious or accidental alteration of data in a database or system. Contamination of data leads to poorer quality data that has low integrity. Thus, data contamination reduces our confidence in the utility of a statistical model; it cannot be trusted for the purpose of analytics-driven decision-making.

Often a solution to these problems involves continuous mining of data streams, such as network traffic monitoring, fraud detection, and even market trend analysis. In all, three fundamental issues are at the center of this problem:[2]

---

1 Mann, M. E., & Lees, J. M. (1996). Robust estimation of background noise and signal detection in climatic time series. *Climatic Change, 33*, 409–445.

2 Chu, F., Wang, Y., & Zaniolo, C. (2006). An adaptive learning approach for noisy data streams. Retrieved from http://web.cs.ucla.edu/~zaniolo/papers/chuf_adaptive.pdf.

- *Adaptation Issue.* To alleviate problems associated with concept drift, statistical models must be adaptive and update routinely to ensure that analytics models optimize decision-making.
- *Robustness Issue.* It can be difficult to distinguish noise from changes caused by concept drift. It is therefore important that efforts to adapt a statistical model are not too liberal (leading to false positives; i.e., actions that are incorrect) or too conservative (leading to false negatives; i.e., not taking actions that should have been taken).
- *Performance Issue.* An important feature of any analytics capability is the ability to perform analytics across vast data sets, such that models can be adapted in real time, with adequate infrastructure and resources.

With a big data information surge, HCOs have the critical task of distinguishing actionable data (i.e., the signal) from noise. Actionable data enables effective decision-making that can answer questions not only about "what is known" (descriptive analytics), but also "how to predict it" (predictive analytics) and "what to do about it" (prescriptive analytics). It is therefore vital to develop adaptive, robust analytics models with a suitable data infrastructure to support analytics performance. Ultimately, aligning actionable data with analytics modeling is crucial to maximize performance, both in terms of HCOs and driving value for patients.

ALIGNING DATA WITH PROCESSES

The need for aligning data with processes is essential and is consistently ranked among top priorities for business intelligence capabilities.[3] Examples of alignment that are applied across the 6 Ps include the following:

- updating information and databases
- developing automated processes
- avoiding information silos
- streamlining data retrieval procedures
- identifying protocols for data analysis

A key aim for any alignment of data with processes is to follow the principle of *parsimony*: Keep it as simple as possible. From a data technology point of view, this means establishing automated tools across the data life cycle to ensure that processes are efficient and can be consistently utilized across an enterprise. Establishing an effective framework for aligning data with processes is called enterprise architecture, which is a conceptual blueprint that

3 Wang, X., Ma, F., & Zhou, X. (2008). Aligning business and IT using enterprise architecture. *Proceedings of the international conference on wireless communications, networking and mobile computing*, WiCOM, pp 1–5. doi: 10.1109/WiCom.2008.2802.

- defines the structure and operation of an organization or entity and
- analyzes processes to determine future plans for effectively achieving strategic objectives.

The ultimate objective for enterprise architecture is to optimize the utility of data across an enterprise. Tracking what data are collected, where it is stored, how it can be found, and if it is retrievable are all important aspects of the enterprise architecture blueprint. In large part, the objective is to determine the degree of coherence between data and its use across an enterprise. This requires comparing the dimensions of data across an enterprise using heuristic rules to detect symptoms of misalignment (same as a doctor identifies symptoms in an ill patient). Thus, enterprise architecture is a malleable, adaptive, continuous learning approach for aligning data with processes. Some examples of key questions asked to ensure alignment between data and process include the following:[4]

- Is there redundancy in business processes and information assets?
- Are there processes that make no access to any entity, and are there entities that are not accessed by any process?
- Who are responsible for generating the data, entering and storing the data, and managing retrieval and query processes?
- What type of data is stored (e.g., numeric, alphanumeric), and how is it stored?
- Are data quality standards and performance goals for an organization or entity being met?

To optimize decision-making, it is important that the data inputs for the analytics models employed actually reflect what is happening in practice. For this reason, it is vital that analytics experts communicate closely with businesses and professionals to ensure that analytics models optimally inform effective organizational decision-making. While there must be a connection between data and decisions, communication among analysts and business professionals is equally vital to ensure that decisions made at an enterprise level can be trusted.

IDENTIFYING TRIGGERS AND INDICATORS FOR PERFORMANCE

Aligning data with processes is important, and sometimes it can help to work backwards to optimize a data plan. This means driving value in analytics models by connecting desired outcomes to *quality* of care, *access* to care, and *costs*

[4] Castellanos, C., & Correal, D. (2013). A framework for alignment of data and processes architectures applied in a government institution. *Journal on Data Semantics,* 2(2–3), 61–74. doi: 10.1007/s13740-013-0021-5.

of care. Figure 13.1 illustrates a triangular model for connecting analytics to each of the fundamental performance outcomes that are vital to driving value in health care. The key performance outcomes of quality, access, and cost were first illustrated in the pentagonal framework in Figure 1.1 in Chapter 1.

To meet performance standards and outcome goals it is fundamentally important to predict changes at all levels of data (indicators) and to utilize data to identify decision points (triggers). Indicators are used to predict shifts or changes over time. Triggers are decision points, or inflection points, where data indicate the need for decisions to be made (i.e., where data demands action). That said, indicators can certainly lead to the need for decisions to be made, but not always. Amalgamated, indicators and triggers guide decision-making along a continuum of care, from the health of an HCO (business health) to the health of the patients they serve (clinical health).

To delineate the value of indicators from triggers, it is important to consider the use of *thresholds* for indicators and triggers to provide clarity. Thresholds for indicators and triggers should be

- *measurable* (i.e., cholesterol is measured in milligrams (mg) of cholesterol per deciliter (dL) of blood)
- *defined* (i.e., total cholesterol scores are considered good at 200 mg/dL or below, borderline from 200 to 239 mg/dL, and high at 240 mg/dL or above); and
- *actionable* (i.e., higher cholesterol levels above 200 mg per dL lead to medication or behavioral changes).

Triggers and indicators are often used to check the health of an organization in business settings and the health of patients in clinical settings. They provide clues into possible adverse events or events that could be harmful.[5] Measuring the overall level of harm across the business and clinical ends of the healthscape taxonomy (see Figure 2.1, Chapter 2) is vital to organizational and patient health, respectively. The use of triggers and indicators at a clinical level, for example, can guide physicians to more effectively identify events that cause harm to patients. In turn, physicians can select and test changes aimed at reducing harm, whether the changes are to processes (e.g., testing protocols) or to diagnosis (e.g., detecting disease).

The utility of identifying triggers and indicators varies depending on performance *thresholds* and can be thought of as programmatic in terms of

- identifying and examining potential indicators, or "risk factors";
- defining trigger points, "cut offs," or causes for immediate action; and
- determining strategies and best courses of action.

[5] Institute of Medicine. (2013). Crisis standards of care: A toolkit for indicators and triggers. Retrieved from https://www.nap.edu/read/18338/chapter/4. doi: 10.17226.18338.

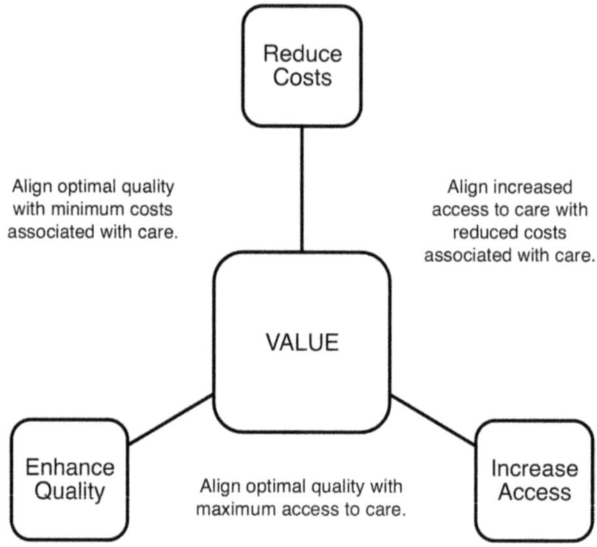

Figure 13.1 Triangulating Value to Key Performance Outcomes.

Same as aligning data with processes, it can be helpful to work backwards by starting with determining strategies and courses of action from which you can enumerate indicators and triggers. In other words, knowing what you are looking for can facilitate your ability to effectively identify the triggers and indictors that would be most valuable to deciding the best courses of action to implement. In addition, it is also important to define *who* handles and analyzes the data, and *who* acts on that information, such as when information requires action in real time (e.g., adapting ER staffing and other resources in response to a crisis). In this way, aligning triggers and indicators with best courses of action is essential to maximizing performance, both in terms of HCOs and driving value for patients.

THINKING OUTSIDE THE BOX: DATA-DRIVEN DECISION-MAKING

Puneet Chahal, Podiatric Surgeon, Olean Podiatry, PC

Data-driven decision-making, or evidence-based medicine, as it pertains to health care, is an increasingly common approach to patient care. Evidence-based medicine is now both accepted and expected when providing treatment. While evidence-based medicine is not a new concept, it is becoming critical in the changing context of health care. With the ever-rising costs of health care, utilizing treatments that have solid efficacy studies supporting their use is crucial to providing streamlined care that is both cost-effective and medically sound. In my specialty of Podiatric Medicine and Surgery, I utilize evidence-based medicine on a daily basis. One of the most common conditions I treat is diabetic foot ulcer. These painful wounds can ultimately lead to loss of limb if not treated properly and aggressively. Evidence-based medicine supports specific evaluation and treatment protocols that help clinicians manage and treat patients suffering with diabetic foot ulcers. The protocols are designed with the goal of minimizing the risk of limb loss. In my practice, I first assess and treat any infection associated with the wound/ulcer. I then assess and manage any underlying vascular insufficiency or disease (i.e., diabetes). The next step typically involves off-loading the wound/ulcer to facilitate proper healing. By following this protocol, I can feel confident that my patients are being treated in a way that is solution-focused with evidence-based data to support its use.

DELINEATING STATISTICAL EFFECTS FOR DECISION-MAKING

Often, you hear the phrase "analytics *informs* decision-making." However, what information is actually conveyed using analytics? How are decision makers informed in a way that strengthens decision-making compared to decisions made without analytics? At a macro-level, analytics provides four levels of information that each answer a fundamental question for decision makers, as also summarized in Figure 13.2:

- *Significance*. Is there an effect in the population?
- *Effect size*. What is the size of the effect in the population?
- *Confidence intervals*. Where is the effect likely to be in the population?
- *Power*. What is the likelihood of detecting the effect, if it exists?

When properly understood, answering each of these questions can substantially bolster the reliability and validity of decisions made across an enterprise. Let us look at each level of information and how it informs decision-making.

Significance

For decision-making using significance, the goal is to determine if effects exist in a population. An *effect* is any discrepancy between what is stated by a null hypothesis and what is actually observed in data that is tested. To make sense of significance, consider a basic courtroom analogy.

Decision-making with analytics follows a similar logic to that in a courtroom. In a courtroom, we begin with the presumption of innocence, and a trial is held to test that presumption. We need some criterion or tipping point where the discrepancy between the presumption of innocence and the evidence of guilt is so great that we will reject the presumption. In a criminal court, the criterion is "beyond reasonable doubt." The decision is ultimately that we disproved this presumption (Decision: Guilty) or that the evidence was not sufficient to disprove it (Decision: Not Guilty).

Likewise, we use the same logic for significance. Here, we begin with the presumption that there is no effect in a population and an analytics model is established to test that presumption. We need some criterion or tipping point where the discrepancy between a null hypothesis and the data is so great that we will reject the null hypothesis. Using analytics, the standard criterion is $p < .05$. Strictly interpreted, this refers to the likelihood of observing an effect, if the null hypothesis were true. If the likelihood of observing an effect is less than or equal to 5 percent, if the null were true, then we reject the null hypothesis (Decision: There is an effect in the population); if the likelihood is greater than 5 percent, if the null were true, then we retain the null hypothesis (Decision: There is no effect in the population).

The effects of interest in health care will vary across the business and clinical ends of the healthscape taxonomy. From revenue and compliance, to wellness and diagnosis outcomes, analytics can identify effects across these domains, and do so with high certainty that these effects truly exist. Utilizing analytics therefore bolsters the confidence of decision makers that their data-driven decisions will lead to desired outcomes across the 6 Ps.

Effect Size

While significance informs decision makers about whether or not an effect exists, effect size adds information about the size of an observed effect. There are generally two ways in which effect size is measured:

- *a change or shift in the population,* typically reported in standard deviation units (e.g., a seasonal promotion during a blood drive increased the number of donors at the event 0.50 standard deviations above expected rates)
- *a proportion or percentage of variance accounted for,* typically reported as a proportion from 0 to 1.0 or as a percentage from 0 to 100 percent (e.g., 8 percent of the variance in patient satisfaction scores can be accounted for by having adequate staffing during high traffic hours)

Effect size is most meaningful for significant effects where the decision was to reject the null hypothesis (i.e., there is an effect). If an effect is not

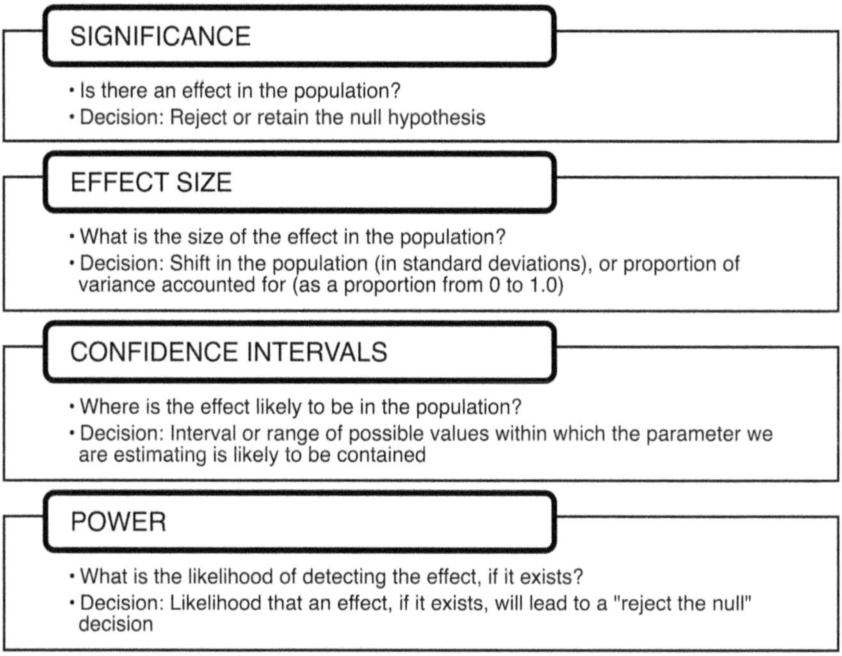

Figure 13.2 Delineating Significance, Effect Size, Confidence Intervals, and Power.

significant, then we decided that an effect does not exist in a population. It therefore makes little sense to measure effect size for an effect that we just concluded does not exist. That said, effect size is a valuable measure in analytics. Knowing the size of observed effects, for example, can inform patients which effects on their health they should pay most attention to, and can inform HCOs where to optimally allocate resources for effects that impact business the most.

Confidence Intervals

In addition to knowing if an effect exists, and the size of the effect, it is also valuable to know where the effect is likely to be. The goal is to estimate within a specified level of confidence, where an effect is likely to be in a population. Using estimation, we state a confidence interval (CI), within which we can be confident that a population parameter is contained. The most common confidence intervals are stated at a 95 percent CI and 99 percent CI level. Estimates are typically reported as a *point estimate* plus or minus an *interval estimate*. This is commonly observed in election polling where candidates are stated as earning 53 percent ± 3 percent of the vote. The following is the conventional decision rule for confidence intervals:

- If a value falls within a confidence interval, then it is likely to be represented in the population.
- If a value falls outside a confidence interval, then it is unlikely to be represented in a population.

The informativeness of confidence intervals is evident anytime there are specific criteria or standards that must be met. For example, a pharmaceutical company may need to confirm that the dosage amount in milligrams (mg) falls within industry standards for a new drug on the market. Suppose the dosage should be at 100 mg. To check this dosage, they sample the dosages for drugs being produced and find with 95 percent confidence that the dosages fall between 98 mg and 101 mg. In this case, 100 mg falls within the confidence interval, so we can conclude that the new drugs are meeting industry guidelines.

Two key features of confidence intervals stand out that impact decision-making, and the following conventions are often used:

- The *precision* of an estimate is determined by the range of the confidence interval. The smaller the range of the interval, the more precise the estimate.
- The *certainty* of an estimate is determined by the level of confidence. The larger the level of confidence, the more certain the estimate.

One implication of the precision and certainty of an estimate is that increasing the level of confidence increases the certainty of an estimate. For this reason, the convention is to use higher levels of confidence in favor of precision. Thus, 95 percent, 99 percent, or larger CIs are most commonly used to guide decision-making across the 6 Ps.

Power

An important caveat for the use of analytics to inform decision makers of effects in a population is that even if an effect exists, it is not a guarantee that the effect will be detected. As a simple analogy, consider a picture where there are 20 hidden images that we are asked to detect. For one picture, the 20 hidden images are large and easy to see; thus, we have high likelihood of detecting or finding all 20 images in the picture. In a second picture, however, the images are much smaller and more difficult to see; thus, we have a lower likelihood of detecting or finding all 20 images in the picture. While there are 20 images in both pictures, one picture is associated with a greater likelihood of detecting those images. If we consider the images to be our "effects" that we are trying to detect, then, the power of the decision-making process is a measure of the likelihood of detecting these effects, if they exist.

In analytics, power is the likelihood that an effect, if it exists, will lead to a decision to "reject the null hypothesis." This is most relevant when samples are used to make decisions because the size of the sample should be sufficient to ensure that effects can be detected, if they exist. The minimal standard for power is .80, meaning that analysts want to make sure that the sample size chosen is large enough to ensure that at least 80 percent of the samples selected will show the effect, if it exists in a population. Power is valuable in terms of its relationship with effect size and sample size:

- Power increases as effect size increases. The larger the effect (or based on our analogy, the larger the "hidden" images are in the picture), the greater the power we will have to detect those effects.
- Power increases as sample size increases. The larger the sample size (or based on our analogy, the greater the number of times we can view the picture), the greater the power we will have to detect those effects.

Of course, as we increase sample size, we incur greater costs associated with sampling and analysis. The costs associated with sampling data tend to be the greatest constraint to ensuring adequate power to detect effects. For this reason, analysts try to balance costs with increasing power by compromising to ensure a minimal standard for power is .80, as stated earlier.

The reason increasing sample size increases power in the first place is because it reduces error. For example, imagine a population has 100 data points. If we sample 10 data points or we sample 90 data points, which sample will do a better job of informing us about the population? The larger sample will, of course. In terms of error, the larger sample is associated with less *error* or variability between what we observe in the sample and what is true in the population. We discuss error in the next section.

ERROR AS A PROXY FOR UNCERTAINTY

Analytics drives decision-making, in part, because of the certainty it can provide, even in the face of uncertainty, which is inevitable. Whether decisions are made at the business or the clinical end of the healthscape taxonomy (see Figure 2.1, Chapter 2), there is almost always some degree of uncertainty in the decisions being made. Markets can change, operational expenses can vary, or standard tests of patient health can lead to false positives or false negatives. The value of analytics is largely driven by its ability to meaningfully measure uncertainty, which in statistical circles is called *error* or *statistical error*. Error is not literally an "error" or a "mistake." Instead, it is any variability that is not attributed to an effect, and can provide critical feedback about random variability that results from data upon which decisions are made.

From a practical perspective, analytics aims to detect effects in the population, upon which decision makers can take action. To do this, all analytics models have to pull apart the sources of variability associated with the to-be-detected effects, and the error variability associated with random variation that occurs simply because some variability is expected even when there are no effects. In reality, some degree of uncertainty will be associated with any decision inasmuch as uncertainty is often inevitable. By accounting for this random variability and controlling for it in models aimed at detecting effects, we can be more certain that effects revealed using analytics models are true effects, and not just random variation, as measured using statistical error. In this way, statistical error is quite informative and can strengthen the certainty of decisions made across the 6 Ps.

BEYOND INFERENTIAL STATISTICS: BIG DATA AND THE LAW OF LARGE NUMBERS

Big data is associated with population-scale data sets that lead to more accurate analyses and thus, by extension, more accurate decision-making. In part, this is due to the law of large numbers, which explains that larger data sets contain greater information, leading to smaller statistical error. With big data, the data sets are so large that the error is almost negligible and thus big data has substantial power to detect effects in a population. The ultimate way to reduce error and maximize the *certainty* of decisions is to boost the size of data to almost the size of the population. This is the "power" of big data—by including such vast, population-scale data in analytics models, even the smallest effects can be detected because the power is so strong and the statistical error is so small. Combining analytics with big data solutions is vital to minimizing uncertainty in decision-making.

Looking ahead, big data is a big solution for issues of significance (Is there an effect?), effect size (How large is the effect?), confidence intervals (Where is the effect?), power (If an effect exists, how likely is it to be detected?), and statistical error (How much random variability is associated with decisions made?). These are fundamental parts of the utility of analytics for driving effective decision-making. Of course, big data comes at a cost, with vital resources needed to support a data infrastructure capable of handling and utilizing such vast data sets. However, even without big data capabilities, it is evident that analytics provides powerful solutions, with its ability to pull apart sources of variability associated with to-be-detected effects and to control for the error variability associated with random variation.

REFERENCES

Castellanos, C., & Correal, D. (2013). A framework for alignment of data and processes architectures applied in a government institution. *Journal on Data Semantics, 2*(2–3), 61–74. doi: 10.1007/s13740-013-0021-5.

Chu, F., Wang, Y., & Zaniolo, C. (2006). An adaptive learning approach for noisy data streams. Retrieved from http://web.cs.ucla.edu/~zaniolo/papers/chuf_adaptive.pdf.

Institute of Medicine. (2013). Crisis standards of care: A toolkit for indicators and triggers. Retrieved from https://www.nap.edu/read/18338/chapter/4. doi: 10.17226.18338.

Mann, M. E., & Lees, J. M. (1996). Robust estimation of background noise and signal detection in climatic time series. *Climatic Change, 33*, 409–445.

Wang, X., Ma, F., & Zhou, X. (2008). Aligning business and IT using enterprise architecture. *Proceedings of the international conference on wireless communications, networking and mobile computing*, WiCOM, pp. 1–5. doi: 10.1109/WiCom.2008.2802.

Chapter 14

Making Health Care Smarter

ECOSYSTEM PERSPECTIVE

The health-care ecosystem continues to be under competitive, financial, political, and regulatory pressures to deliver improved quality, access, and cost. How to do this? As we have discussed, analytics, along with several key supporting technologies and tools, offers one of the best pathways for patients, governments, and HCOs to deliver greater value in our health-care ecosystem and understand the relative clinical value of different health-care services and products. Analytics (i.e., the systematic analysis of data) provides essential information relating to the quality and cost of patient care in ambulatory and non-ambulatory settings. The positive news is that significant quantities of patient and HCO data are continuously generated. The challenge is that much of this data continues to be underutilized or misused. In this chapter we review and extend the discussion of how the 6 Ps as a collective can create increased opportunities to leverage analytics and data in clinical and diagnostic situations to make health care smarter.

Data analytics is increasingly moving beyond either hope or hype as it completely transforms past business paradigms. In many ways, data will be the next great breakthrough for health care. Data can help the 6 Ps do amazing things, and the possibilities are practically unlimited. Health care can be an economic development tool. Healthy people are better contributors as community members, family members, and employees. However, analytics requires people, processes, organizational structure, tools, and technology, and there is substantial detailed, foundational work that must be completed before data becomes reliable and actionable. The lack of analytic capability is one of the biggest bottlenecks that providers and the other Ps face. Yet, given the increasing focus on patient health outcomes, the 6 Ps find it more important than ever to integrate and understand data via smart analytics, which leads to smarter health care.

EVOLUTION IN THE ROLE OF EACH P

Economic, demographic, and technological forces are transforming health care. For the last several decades, the cost of health care has far outpaced the rate of inflation and is expected to consume in excess of 20 percent of US gross domestic product in coming years. The triple aim of health care is to improve patient experience, improve population health, and reduce costs.[1] Of all the 6 Ps, policy makers have played the most catalytic role, encouraging initiatives such as interoperability standards, pattern recognition programs, and personalized care to address these aims. However, there are three powerful demographic trends in health care that will continue to challenge the 6 Ps: (1) increasing shortage of primary care physicians, (2) growth in the percentage of elderly, and (3) increasing incidences of chronic disease, particularly diabetes, high blood pressure, and kidney disease. Shortages in primary care physicians and nurses are triggering a workforce restructuring. The current health-care workforce is trained and the health-care system is structured to treat acute, episodic interventions (e.g., ERs), but chronic diseases are increasing in frequency, giving rise to certain medical "hotspots" in terms of costs.

The health-care ecosystem is working to better align coverage, quality and value-based care, including syncing up of benefits, delivery system, and payment reform. To do this, there will need to be improved care coordination cutting across organizational boundaries, with analytics playing a featured role. Some of the 6 Ps still depend on legacy reporting capabilities of basic business intelligence tools and, even with that, only utilize them sporadically. Other organizations leverage sophisticated enterprise data processing architecture to develop patient-specific insight with regard to every episode of care. Effective analytics requires executives having a scalable data governance roadmap. IT architectures are often misaligned with current clinical goals, so it is important for all of the Ps in the health-care ecosystem to have scorecards on performance and progress to optimize patient outcomes and incentive payments.

Over time, payers—particularly CMS—are forcing more providers to attribute a higher proportion of net revenue to patient outcomes, especially at the aggregate, population level. Thus, analytics investments will need to be tied to population health management. While there will be overlaps, the objective of analytics for one P will differ from that of another P. For example, providers

1 Berwick, D. M., Nolan, T.W., & Whittington, J. (2008). The triple aim: Care, health, and cost. *Health Affairs. May/June, 27*(3), 759–769. doi: 10.1377/hithaff.27.3.759.

can leverage analytics for the identification, evaluation, and benchmarking of cost trends across different mixes of patients, physicians, and payers. In slight contrast, payers can leverage analytics to highlight evidence-based, quality-adjusted target costs and prices for each episode of care. Ecosystem partners will need to be flexible in responding to changing market needs. For instance, payers, pharmacists, and pharmaceuticals are moving to the inner clinical circle. Some payers think of themselves as analytics/IT companies and data partners for providers rather than insurance companies. The fee-for-service model was largely zero-sum and pitted payers against providers, but more than ever, payers now want to help providers perform better. Because of higher deductibles and premiums, more and more patients are taking on a more significant payer role. So, all the Ps will need to be flexible as the boundaries among them continue to evolve.

BENEFITS TO PATIENTS OF SMARTER HEALTH CARE

Smarter health care is a patient-centric, innovation-focused ecosystem where analytics and data are used to integrate the 6 Ps across the care continuum and the transition from volume- to value-based care has been fully realized. Patients should be engaged and empowered, and we are moving toward accessible, highly personalized, and on-time health-care services. New technologies provide patients with opportunities to take more responsibility for their own health and wellness. Resources provided to patients can include clinical staff chat, disease management education, online health screenings, and text message alerts/reminders. Many patients do not have a good grasp on the basics of their health insurance, including what services are covered and the level of the deductible, so we also need smarter health-care consumers.

Key components of creating a better patient experience are access, affordability, convenience, and quality. One broad goal is to increase patient access to care providing strong clinical value. Patient-centered engagement is increasingly becoming person-centered engagement which holistically aims to treat the entire human being. The patient-centered medical home (PCMH) is a model that focuses on primary care, including ongoing wellness, and on creating a long-term relationship between patients and providers. As part of establishing a "home" for patients, the PCMH team closely tracks the patient's condition. Those with a primary care physician or some medical base/home have a higher probability of participating in preventative measures and wellness initiatives.

In terms of patient benefit, the IoT, which is inherently smart technologically, becomes particularly useful for patients who are elderly, have chronic conditions, or require constant supervision. From the comfort of their homes, patients can chat online with clinical personnel, complete data gathering tasks, and assess/respond to wellness gaps in care. Goal-oriented wellness tasks, remote monitoring, and health journaling can be used to empower and engage patients. Using historical data, patients can review and assess their own medical history, allowing them to track progress against goals.

One challenge is delivering better, smarter health care via remote patient monitoring. Remote patient monitoring holds opportunities to deliver innovative digital services and grow new markets, but the future growth in managing patients via remote monitoring requires greater automation, effective end-to-end view of service performance, and of course, improved outcomes and quality of service. When there are serious symptoms (e.g., unexpected or unexplained changes in blood pressure, glucose levels, or heart rate), remote monitoring can provide patients at home—and their institution-based providers—with early warning signs. This reduces the time patients need to spend in the hospital and decreases readmissions. Patients can conduct a number of activities online to better manage their health care, including having chat sessions with a clinical professional, requesting referrals, making appointments, and setting goals. Less staff support is needed when patients use online communication tools. This all makes for smarter health care and smarter patients.

MULTI-SECTOR TECHNOLOGY AND TOOLS

In this section, we examine many of the technologies and tools that are making health care smarter across the 6 Ps. The past ad hoc collection of tools could not consistently get administrators and practitioners clear, comprehensive answers, and when that finally did happen, so much time may have passed to make the data obsolete (i.e., the set of tools was not smart enough to deliver what was needed when). There needs to be a capability to drill down to individual level data. Traditional, relational database platforms and technologies are not equipped to process the huge volume of unstructured data found in clinical notes, digital devices, imaging, laboratory tests, telematics, and many other sources. Even a data field of 25 columns and millions of rows may only be able to hold three weeks of data from an active surgery center. In some cases, to achieve actionable insights from data, the organization needs to purchase add-on analytics products, and this extra step often dissuades use.

There should be comprehensive clinical support software. The healthcare data analytics platform is a single, interoperable system leveraging descriptive and retrospective data to generate business intelligence analyses quantifying enterprise-level dimensions of key financial and operational performance indicators, while also utilizing multisource clinical data on each episode of care to produce predictive analyses and real-time assessments. Platform-based products are built using clinical decision support systems,

EHRs, population health management data, and revenue cycle management. This software enables smarter use of data.

The frequently mentioned IoT is another key tool. The IoT market is now vast, while being increasingly mission critical and allowing organizations to achieve greater reliability and scalability. Powered by virtual, wired, real-time sense and response capabilities embedded in objects, the IoT is providing smart data. Intelligent health-care devices capture data via built-in sensors. Key related tools in smart care are the AI, cloud, machine learning, RFID, sensors, and wearable technologies. IBM Watson is an example of AI that applies automated analytics and reasoning to complement human evaluation in identifying patterns and anomalies. Machine learning is centered on discovering new knowledge and providing intelligence based on emerging data rather than just on pre-derived, embedded data. RFID tags can be used to track the medications of individual patients. RFID can help improve logistics management and reduce inventory costs. Other key innovations include 3D printing and robotics. Eventually, many people in the 6 Ps will have robotic personal assistants. There are now smart bandages, smart pills, smart syringes, and technology enabling remote surgeries.

New mobile technology platforms facilitate innovative ways to coordinate care delivery by providing a holistic view of the patient, and the increasing smartphone penetration rates is helping drive mobile health. Providers and their technology vendors can now implement cross-device connectivity and smart features as a core component of medical devices and related software systems. New proof-of-concept projects are continually being launched that test real-world service delivery and technology use scenarios. Even as the scope of the technology widens, in order to ensure quality of care, providers will need to allocate network services in an automated, dynamic, and flexible way in conjunction with specified medical devices and monitors.

Another trend is remote monitoring of the healing process. Connected, smart devices, including multiple biometric monitors, can be utilized to support home-based care, precision care, and preventive care. The communications infrastructure and technology services serving as the basis for remote monitoring are rapidly growing in maturity and sophistication. Leveraging disparate devices, remote patient monitoring, including continual evaluation of how a wound is healing, can be effective in providing many service levels on one virtualized network.

One aspect that is decidedly not smart about our current health-care system is the failure of patients to take their medications (i.e., nonadherence or noncompliance). This is a major public health problem, but it is also amenable to change with the use of smart technology and tools. For example, currently on the market, there is a smart pill bottle product that records when a bottle cap is opened and closed. Although it is possible for a patient to "game the system" by opening the container but not consuming any of the contents, the bottle does allow for insight about whether a patient has remembered to take a medication. This product also includes an app that reminds patients when it is time to take a pill, including follow-up phone calls and texts if the patient does not respond. In addition, when it is time to medicate, the cap blinks an LED and makes a noise. To avoid double dosing, the app will send a warning if the pill bottle is opened again too soon after the patient has last opened the bottle. Other vendors offer products that can measure the actual level of contents inside the bottle. A smart bottle is an example of a tool that can benefit all the 6 Ps in various ways:

- Patients reap the health benefits of taking the right medicine in the right dosage at the right time.
- Policy makers see public health (as an aggregate of the individual medication adherent patients) improve.
- Providers, with healthier patients, can report better outcomes, which is crucial for reimbursement given the shift from volume to value.
- Pharmacies have to deal with fewer complications from medication nonadherence.
- Pharmaceuticals experience boosted metrics on drug effectiveness, which is important for reimbursement.
- Payers see reduced health-care costs overall as a natural result of patients adhering to their drug regimens.

Cognitive computing, which is an essential driver for many of these tools, incorporates deep learning and machine learning, but it extends that to derive true insights. The discipline of cognitive computing includes AI, machine learning, and deep learning. Smarter health care will require smarter algorithms. Rather than replacing physicians or scientists, AI and related tools can be the ultimate research assistant, augmenting human decision-making. Of course, by itself, smart technology cannot serve as a complete and comprehensive solution. Technology is an enabler, but ultimately people and processes will drive improved care. Once fully taught and trained, which takes years, cognitive computing models can quickly generate insights on patient health. The growth of IoT is limited by the need for high capital investments and still poor overall awareness levels among consumers/patients. Thus, technology and tools are only part of the equation as the 6 Ps create smart, analytics-driven health care.

PROCESSING DATA BY THE 6 Ps

Before data can be leveraged to build smarter health care, it must be properly sourced and processed. Major data buckets include administrative, claims,

EHR, laboratory, and pharmacy. More specific sources of data include adverse events reporting, clinical records, clinical trials, diagnostics, EHRs genetic data, imaging, probes, sensors, and wearables. There is also a huge volume of digital genome data flowing into the health-care ecosystem, especially for pharmaceuticals and providers. Creating standard data definitions and vocabularies is crucial for standardizing the integration process, particularly when data is sourced from different components of the same enterprise or from different enterprises. The system should standardize, integrate, and place data in a secure location. Claims, EHR, and laboratory data should all be aggregated and deposited into a centralized repository (i.e., a data warehouse). For purposes of performance scoring and reporting, it is important to have automated XML file creation drawn from a data repository. Entities can create central repositories to store all patient data and then leverage AI to address gaps in post-acute care.

For data to effectively strengthen clinical and strategic decision-making, it must be trusted by users, whether they are patients, administrators/executives, physicians, nurses, pharmacists, actuaries, or data scientists. Misleading data begets inaccurate decision-making. Thus, reliability and validity must be established throughout the data value continuum. Data must be protected from breach, corruption, or loss and should be cleaned, converted, and collated to become understandable to an algorithm. Throughout the data acquisition, collection, and integration sequence, there should be data audits and quality assurance controls. Particularly in the past, data cleanup was done manually, but this data janitorial work is costly and time-consuming, requiring lots of human capital.

As the analytics market matures, quality reporting will become essential for population health management and value-based care. HCOs can leverage risk stratification to create effective population management, decrease system waste, and prioritize clinical workflow, and providers are designing data asset strategies. There needs to be a data science strategy, and it should cover the complete data value continuum—from acquisition to utilization. The 6 Ps individually and collectively must aim to refine best practices for the design, development, deployment, and governance of analytics solutions regarding clinical, financial, and operational data because there is relatively low interoperability between existing and emerging IT solutions. At the enterprise level, this presents a significant hurdle to harmonize, normalize, and source disparate patient data. Future analytics solutions should connect siloed departments while remaining highly scalable.

In order to make smarter decisions, executives need to gain deeper visibility into procedures and processes. Analytics need to be embedded into the complex workflows of health care, including how data is created, captured, organized, curated, and analyzed. Ease of access to data should be at the heart of an organization's digital framework, and there should be documentation on intervention in operational workflows. For example, the EHR should not only contain an accurate and comprehensive profile for the patient but also the provenance of the information. In addition, because data is only as useful as the insights it generates, there should be strategic planning about how data is going to be used on the back end.

LEVERAGING DATA BY THE 6 Ps

Smart data processing sets the foundation for smart data leveraging, which includes analytics and technology. Analytics applications include administrative systems, clinical domain expertise, large-scale integrations, patient portals, and biopharmaceutical research and development. Technology applications include population health management, patient case management, and patient risk stratification, as well as asset management, environmental monitoring, patient flow, and staff flow.

When thinking about risk stratification, it is important to identify high-risk, low-risk, and rising-risk categories. In addition to population risk assessment and quality reporting, other significant growth opportunities for analytics include administrative automation, clinical asset utilization, clinical surveillance, precision medicine, revenue cycle management, and supply chain optimization. There is technology available to help manage commercial, Medicaid, Medicare, and self-insured employer populations. Data can include primary diagnosis, procedure, and provider type, and it is important to have drill down capability with the data to facilitate granularity in the analysis. For example, in the context of a surgical center, a senior executive should be able to pull up data delineating supplies use for patients, with comparisons between days of the week, locations, surgical teams, and outcomes. This can provide deep visibility into cost per patient, supply cost trends, and waste issues.

Analytics can help reduce abuse, fraud, and waste using AI and machine learning to detect anomalies in billing (e.g., costs significantly above regional peer providers, duplicate claims, and unnecessary procedures). Anomaly models can assign risk scores to specific claims, procedures, and providers and, in turn, flag aberrancies that were highly difficult to detect using older manual human-driven models. Fraudulent billers are frequently connected via tight networks, and analytics can discern these social network patterns. A gap analysis can be conducted comparing EHR data imports to claims data, and web-based security risk assessments can be used to identify any compliance gaps.

With regard to the patient specifically, smart analytics can automate risk assessment, facilitate targeted intervention, and drive proactive member outreach. The goal should be to attain a 360-degree, holistic view of patients. Analytics can help prevent some of the adverse events, particularly avoidable medical errors, which kill thousands of patients annually. Nonetheless, proactive alerting is crucial. The presence or worsening of several conditions (e.g., asthma, diabetes, heart failure, pneumonia, and urinary tract infections) is amenable to detection using real-time analytics.

Consider some other ways one or more of the 6 Ps can leverage data to become smarter:

- Analyze bundled payments and episodes of care.
- Customize logistics, transport, and warehousing.
- Deliver evidence-based personalized medicine.
- Eliminate preventable costs.
- Facilitate per member per month data to identify improvement opportunities, enhance capacity planning, and aid long-term budgeting.
- Manage operating room costs, schedule refinements, and quality improvement procedures.
- Improve drug discovery, hospital workflow, medical imaging and diagnosis, and therapy planning.

Analytical algorithms are needed to harness big data in the ways listed above. A given patient might stand out based on anomalous combinations of comorbidities and lab results. From a causal perspective, smart data analysis can help tease out differences in outcomes based on variations in provider performance, patient populations, system resources, or other variables. Machine learning has reached a sufficient maturity level that it can begin engaging in diagnoses and predicting medical events with an increasing degree of accuracy. Using de-identified medical records of past patients, advanced machine learning can identify patterns that can then be used to anticipate the needs of specific, identified current patients. A deep learning algorithm can be used, for example, to accurately diagnose diabetic retinopathy or detect cancer spreading to adjacent lymph nodes, and AI can help rapidly identify ER patients with fractures, measure the impact of a stroke, and track the response of tumors to new cancer treatments. The central asset is the algorithm. In this way, the key components of smarter health care can be expressed as a mathematical equation:

Building blocks of smart health care = data + analytics + algorithms + AI

Just as data is the fuel for analytics, ultimately the algorithm is the fuel for AI and machine learning. Together they are the pillars of smarter health care.

THINKING OUTSIDE THE BOX: LEVERAGING ANALYTICS FOR BETTER DECISIONS, BETTER HEALTH

Joseph P. Gaspero, CEO and Cofounder, Center for Healthcare Innovation

Data analytics has the power to fundamentally alter decision-making in health care, as it allows providers and decision makers to make "smarter, quicker, and agile" decisions. Harnessing the power of data, clinicians have more information than ever. And as precision medicine and artificial intelligence loom on the horizon, the amount of data we have and how we leverage it will alter care delivery. However, technology and data analytics are only some of many tools to optimize decision-making. The best care and decisions are made when data is combined with a proper patient engagement and communication strategy. Too often, advances in technology are thought to be "the end all and be all." However, in addition to leveraging technology to make smarter decisions, a strategy that properly combines data analytics with new and novel communication and engagement approaches will lead to the best care outcomes.

ANALYTICS CHALLENGES FOR THE 6 Ps

There are several challenges to making health care smarter. The core enemies of effective data analytics are lack of interoperability, poor IT governance, and insufficient data integrity. Combining data for disparate systems can yield a hodgepodge of information of marginal value. Data migration, transformation, and integration from legacy systems to new systems can pose severe difficulties. Even when technically successful, key contextual and dimensional information can be lost. This makes the operation less clinically successful because analytical algorithms often require that context to fully leverage the data.

EHRs, which should be an unalloyed benefit, actually pose additional challenges. If not properly implemented, clinical documentation and EHR use can result in physicians conducting greater face-to-screen computer work at the expense of face-to-face patient interactions, and these systems can be a source of dysfunction and physician burnout. Why? Key reasons include time required for data input, increased oversight made possible by the data, loss of control of practicing medicine, profound inefficiencies related to interoperability, and poor user interfaces.

Getting access to data continues to be another challenge. Because health care is so highly regulated, there is a significant amount of data that cannot be used. In addition, many HCOs hoard data, and some EHR vendors design systems that make data sharing outside their proprietary platform difficult. In the past, many providers have pursued attempts at IT innovation that proved catastrophic because of overengineering coupled with inattention to human dimensions. Key issues are privacy, security, and veracity. So, as noted earlier, there needs to be clear traceability of information back to the point of inception. Measurements and metrics should be replicable, standardized, timely, and validated.

To improve both the quality of care and the quality of life, more data is needed from multiple sources. Some data is a mile deep and an inch wide (e.g., clinical trial data), and some is a mile wide and an inch deep (e.g., claims data). The goal should be to develop databases for patients that are both deep and wide. A good algorithm is difficult to build, and relationships among data in the real world are complex. The tolerance for error is exceedingly slim as machine learning mistakes could cost someone a life. Machines can learn from only the data that is provided. So, there is a need to harvest ever larger, higher-quality databases to build the best algorithms possible. These improvements will save lives and make people healthier.

SMARTER ANALYTICS

Value is the key output for our health-care ecosystem, and value is a function of the ability of the 6 Ps to collectively deliver quality, affordability, and access. That data analytics is an essential enabler for achieving value is not revelation, but in this book, we delineate the specific roles of the 6 Ps in generating and utilizing data-driven decision models, technologies, and tools that increase quality, increase access, and decrease costs. However, in addition to concrete data and practical tools, the human dimension needs to be the ultimate catalyst for smarter health care.

Effective executive leadership and skilled data analytics talent are two of the greatest challenges facing health-care analytics. With the growth in AI and machine learning, clinical cognitive science is approaching a tipping point. Data is the new standard for operational excellence, and analytics can help the 6 Ps stop throwing darts in the dark. Still, smart leadership is needed to translate analytics into action. Computers are effective at assessing, but currently they do not have the level of reliability we need for high-stake matters requiring careful judgment. That requires human talent. There is likely to be a significant shortage of data scientists in the coming years. In terms of compensation packages, most HCOs cannot compete with banks and other financial services firms. Thus, finding, recruiting, training, and retaining analytic expertise will be a challenge for all HCOs. As part of implementing data analytics, leaders should build in feedback loops and time for reflection to assess the technical landscape. This is not easy because the US health-care analytics market is likely to remain highly fragmented as modular analytics solutions from disparate vendors continue to multiply.

Looking ahead, there should be alignment between an organization's overall strategy and its data governance plan. As with any economic transformation, there will be winners and losers at the individual and organizational levels. However, everyone in the health-care ecosystem has been or will be affected by illness or injury, directly or indirectly. So, analytics ultimately will generate significant value for society as a whole by helping make health care and medicine higher quality, more affordable, and more accessible.

REFERENCE

Berwick, D. M., Nolan, T.W., & Whittington, J. (2008). The triple aim: Care, health, and cost. *Health Affairs. May/June, 27*(3), 759–769. doi: 10.1377/hithaff.27.3.759.

Conclusion

The value of a health-care system is ultimately best measured by the quality, access, and costs associated with patient care. This perspective was at the core of the patient-centric analytics approach taken in this book. While there is a wealth of data available across the spectrum of health care, much of it is not fully utilized. There is a need to optimize the utility of these data, and analytics is the optimal tool to connect data to decision-making that drives *value.*

Value is the key output for the health-care ecosystem, and value is a function of the ability of the 6 Ps to collectively deliver enhanced quality of care, increased access to care, and reduced costs associated with care. In this book, we delineated the unique roles of the 6 Ps and built into this understanding not only the value that can be created using data-driven decision models, technologies, and tools but also how to manage these tools to optimize the use of data to enhance quality, increase access, and decrease costs. More than having concrete data and practical tools, however, we must also be considerate of the critical human dimension of patient care ("patient centricity") for achieving a smarter health-care system.

For the sake of society, health-care productivity needs to increase, which will require taking care of more people with fewer resources. Health care is still highly labor intensive, and over the past couple decades, the sector has demonstrated relatively few productivity gains compared to other components of the economy. Health care urgently requires a productivity revolution. To make that happen, data should be treated as one of the most valuable strategic assets. Throughout this book, we have identified a pentagonal framework from which to identify the vastness of the health-care space, and we have examined the benefits of managing and utilizing data across this space.

A key challenge across the spectrum of health care is not only to deliver value but also to *measure* deliverables in a way that can *show* value. While the interests of the 6 Ps can be quite diverse, there are substantial synergies across the 6 Ps to deliver value to patients—thereby placing patients at the center of the pentagonal framework. As detailed throughout this book, there are a broad range of interests and synergies that can be leveraged to positively impact quality, access, and cost across the health-care ecosystem. The extent to which data can be leveraged using analytics to optimize decision-making may ultimately depend on the ability of the 6 Ps to realize the interests that they share to benefit the central stakeholders in the system: the patients.

Glossary

A1C test: A test used to diagnose diabetes in which an A1C level of greater than 6.5 percent on two different tests indicates the presence of diabetes, and a result in the range from 5.7 percent to 6.4 percent indicates prediabetes, which is an elevated risk of developing diabetes. (6)

Access: Ease at which patients can utilize care in the system. (1)

Accountable Communities for Health (ACHs): A population health–based model that seeks to improve health outcomes and reduce costs by addressing unmet health-related social needs such as community support, food insecurity, inadequate transportation, physical safety, and unstable housing; ACHs are particularly applicable to the management of chronic conditions or degenerative diseases. (6)

Actionable Data: Data that is useful or that can be transformed into information that can be used for making effective decisions or drawing meaningful conclusions. (13)

Algorithms: A set of processes and rules that dictate a certain course of action based on calculations or other problem-solving operations. (7)

Analytics: The systematic analysis of data or statistics to obtain information that has value and can be utilized. (1)

Artificial Intelligence (AI): The application of computer systems and other machines to the performance of tasks such as decision-making, speech recognition, and voice identification that normally require human intelligence. (7)

Big Data: Vast data sets often stored in files so large that they exceed the random access memory (RAM) of a standard computer, that can be analyzed computationally to reveal patterns, trends, and associations used to guide decision-making. (2)

Biomarker: Measurable biological characteristic in a person, the presence of which is suggestive of potential disease, infection, or another medical ailment. (9)

Body Mass Index: A measure for relating weight to height, for which a range of 20–25 is considered normal, a range of 25–30 is considered overweight, and an index greater than 30 is considered obese. (6)

Cluster Sampling: A method of sampling in which subgroups or clusters of individuals are identified in a population, and then a portion of clusters that are representative of the population are selected such that all individuals in the selected clusters are included in the sample. All clusters that are not selected are omitted from the sample. (3, 12)

Comorbidity: Medical situation where a patient simultaneously has two chronic conditions or diseases. (8)

Concept Drift: The change in a target "concept" for which a statistical model is trying to predict that is difficult to anticipate and can create noise, thereby reducing the accuracy of predictions made by a model over time. (13)

Concept Identifier Codes: A comprehensive health-care terminology in words, letters, symbols, synonyms, and definitions to encode meanings to support the effective recording and reporting of data. (4)

Concierge Medical Practice: An innovative service in which a consumer pays, whether on a retainer, membership, or cash-only basis, a physician or group practice to provide care that is enhanced in terms of quality, comprehensiveness, and convenience. (5)

Confidence Interval (CI): The interval or range of possible values within which the parameter we are estimating is likely to be contained. (13)

Consumer: A person who makes decisions on purchasing products and services for personal use. This can be contrasted with a patient, who is the actual user of health-care products and services. (5)

Consumer-Patient-Person (CPP) platform: A new potential software technology platform that integrates benefits information, clinical information, and lifestyle/wellness information in one location for users. (5)

Cost: Expenditures required to make the system efficient. (1)

Cross Industry Standard Process for Data Mining (CRISP-DM): An analytics program that employs six phases: business understanding, data understanding, data preparation, modeling, evaluation, and deployment. (3)

Dashboard: A visual representation of a set of key performance measures. (3)

Data: Measurements, quantities, characters, or symbols that are typically collected for the purpose of analysis at a later stage. (1)

Data Contamination: The malicious or accidental alteration of data in a database or system. (13)

Data Integrity: The validity and trustworthiness of data over its life cycle. (11)

Data Mining: A predictive analytical tool that borrows a lot from descriptive analytics to evaluate patterns and features among variables in large data sets. (3)

Data Modeling: Development of an abstract model that organizes data elements and establishes how they relate to one another and to elements in the real world. (3)

Data Partitioning: The process of randomly splitting a data set into three parts, thereby creating three samples from one larger set, from which one set is used to build the model, the second is used to test it, and the third is used to validate the final model. (3)

Data Quality: The usefulness of data to test, assess, or solve a particular problem for a given purpose. (11)

Data Quality Assurance: A process of verifying the utility of data by identifying inconsistencies and anomalies in data, then filtering the data to improve data quality. (11)

Data Warehouse: A central repository of integrated data from one or more disparate sources that is used for storing, reporting, and analyzing data. (4)

Database: A structured set of data stored in a computer. (3)

Database Management System: A management interface between the database where data are stored and the person who actually uses the data to ensure that data are consistently organized and easily accessible. (11)

Database Query: A request for data or information from a database through which data may be generated as results returned by SQL, or as pictorials, graphs or complex analyses. (3)

Deep Learning: Artificial neural networks consisting of many layers that leverage machine learning for applications to complex and large datasets. (9)

Deliverable: A tangible or intangible output produced by the inputs of a given system or entity. (1)

Dendrogram: A branching, tree diagram that visually delineates causal and taxonomic relationships between variables. (8)

Descriptive Analytics: An analytical approach that describes or summarizes raw data and makes it interpretable or meaningful in order to assess past and current performance and guide decision-making. (1, 3)

DMAIC: An analytics methodology, that when combined with Six Sigma, provides an analytics framework for business to reduce costs and increase quality in five phases: Define, Measure, Analyze, Improve, and Control. (3)

Effect: The discrepancy between assumptions in an analytics model, often stated
in the null hypothesis, and what is observed in data used to test the assumptions. When a null hypothesis is rejected, we decide that an effect exists in a given population. (12, 13)

Effect Size: A measure of the size of an effect in a population that allows analysts to describe a shift in the population, or the proportion of variance accounted for. (13)

Electronic Health Record (EHR): An electronic version of a patient's medical history maintained by a provider over time to automate access to patient workflow information. (Introduction, 1)

Enterprise Architecture: A conceptual blueprint that defines the structure and operation of an organization or entity, and analyzes processes to determine future plans for effectively achieving strategic objectives. (13)

External Reporting: A business practice that involves collecting data or information that is prepared for viewing by the general public or auditors from outside an organization. (4)

Federally Qualified Health Center (FQHC): A special reimbursement designation issued by the Bureau of Primary Health Care and the Centers for Medicare and Medicaid Services of the United States Department of Health and Human Services. FQHCs extend health-care services to all patients regardless of their ability to pay and generally charge based on a sliding-fee scale according to household income and size. (6)

Fee-For-Service (FFS): The dominant health-care reimbursement model in the United States that compensates hospitals, physicians, and other providers based on unbundled services and separate payments; via health insurance coverage, it also generally shields patients from significant cost-sharing. The FFS model is widely seen as rewarding the quantity of care rather than the quality of care. (6)

Forecasting: An analytical strategy for estimating or predicting future business-related outcomes. (3)

Fuzzy Logic: Type of computing based on a continuum and degrees of truth rather than the typical Boolean logic of "true or false" (1 or 0) that usually serves as the basis for the modern computer. (9)

Genomics: Component of molecular biology focused on the evolution, function, mapping, and structure of genomes, which is the entire set of genes or genetic material in a cell. (9)

Health Coach: A professional health-care provider who works with patients, families, and providers to coordinate care across the continuum and to optimize the client's health and wellness. (5)

Health Information Exchange (HIE): The electronic mobilization or exchange of health-care information across organizations within a region, community or hospital system, which allows health-care professionals and patients to appropriately access and securely share vital medical information electronically. (4)

Healthscape: A taxonomy for the health-care space extending from business to clinically related outcomes of interest across the 6 Ps. (2)

Histogram: A graphical display used to summarize the frequency of data that are distributed in numeric intervals. (3)

Indicators: Information that is used to predict shifts or changes in data over time. (13)

Inferential Statistics: Statistical procedures used in business settings to assess known data in a model to make inferences regarding past and current business performance and guide decision-making. (3)

Infodemiology: The capability of patients, providers, payers, and other health-care stakeholders to systematically locate, aggregate, and analyze user-generated data to inform individual decisions, as well as public health and public policy. (5)

Information: Data that are processed, organized, structured, or presented in a meaningful or useful manner. (11)

Internal Reporting: A business practice that involves collecting data or information for internal use to inform decision-makers and stakeholders in an organization. (4)

Internet of Things (IoT): The interconnectivity of numerous everyday objects via embedded computing devices sending, receiving, and processing data through the Internet. (7)

Interoperability: The ability of computer software and systems to meaningfully exchange and utilize data and other information. (7)

Law of Large Numbers: The law that the larger the sample size, the smaller the standard error, and thus the larger the power to detect effects in a population. (12)

Machine Learning: A form of artificial intelligence (AI) representing the ability of computers to self-learn without being explicitly programmed. (7)

Medication Reconciliation: The process of a pharmacist creating a comprehensive list of all the medications a patient is supposed to be taking, including the drug name, dosage, frequency, and administration route (e.g., oral or topical) and then comparing that to all provider records (e.g., discharge orders) to insure the correct medications are being taken. (8)

Metadata: Data that describes or provides information about one or more aspects of other data types. (11)

Metric: A description for a measurement quantified in terms of the specific process or manner by which it was observed or measured. (11)

Next-Generation Sequencing: DNA sequencing technologies allowing billions of DNA strands to be sequenced in parallel; also known as high-throughput sequencing. (9)

Noise: Data that are meaningless, redundant, corrupt, or non-interpretable. (13)

Nonparametric Tests: Procedures used to test data with parameters in a population that are unknown or not normally distributed and measured on an ordinal or nominal scale of measurement. (3)

Opioid: A drug that binds to one or more of the body's three opioid receptors and which can produce a profound physiological impact on patients (8)

Optimization: A prescriptive analytics process of selecting values of *decision variables* (values a model seeks to determine) that minimize or maximize an *object function* (the value we want to maximize or minimize) with appropriate constraints (limitations or restrictions) added to translate the object function and constraints into mathematical expressions that can then be applied to identify optimal solutions to a problem. (3)

Oversampling: A sampling strategy that adjusts up certain types of individuals or data, particularly for characteristics that are more represented in a population. (12)

Parametric Tests: Procedures used to test data with parameters in a population that are normally distributed and measured on an interval or ratio scale of measurement (3)

Patient-Centered Care: An approach to health care where patients actively participate in decision-making regarding their own medical treatment in collaboration with health professionals and where the quality of life, risk-preferences, and values of patients are the primary considerations. (5)

Patient-Centered Medical Home (PCMH): A model of health care that prioritizes patients by providing them with a primary provider that is responsible for addressing the patient's full care continuum of physical and mental needs, including acute care, chronic care, prevention, and wellness. (14)

Pay-For-Performance (PFP): An emergent health-care reimbursement model in the United States that compensates hospitals, physicians, and other providers based on bundled services and fixed, pre-set payments; via co-payments and deductibles, it also generally regards cost-sharing from patients. The PFP model is widely seen as rewarding the quality of care rather than the quantity of care. (6)

Personalized Medicine: The practice of customizing medical care and treatment to the needs of an individual patient. (4)

Population: A set of all individuals, items, or data of interest about which analysts will generalize. (12)

Power: The likelihood that an effect, if it exists, will lead to a decision to "reject the null hypothesis." (13)

Predictive Analytics: An analytical approach used to predict outcomes by examining existing data for patterns or relationships to make inferences forward in time to inform decision-making. (1, 3)

Predictive Modeling: A predictive analytical tool used to "peer into the future" by transforming inputs into output data that is used to predict which outputs will occur. (3)

Prescriptive Analytics: An analytical approach that integrates descriptive and predictive analytics to find the best course of action for a given situation by (a) entering existing data as inputs, then (b) feeding the outputs back into the system as inputs to update the model to inform decision-making. (1, 3)

Probability: The likelihood that an outcome will occur. (3)

Probability Sampling: A sampling procedure in which all samples of a given size are equally likely to be selected from a larger population data set. (3, 12)

Psychographic: Information related to a person's attitudes, behavior, interests, lifestyles personality, opinions, and values. (10)

Quality: A standard or degree of excellence of care. (1)

Radio Frequency Identification (RFID): A technology that uses electromagnetic or electrostatic coupling in the radio frequency portion of the electromagnetic spectrum to specifically identify an object. (8)

Regression Analysis: A statistical tool used to (a) identify the function that best "fits" the pattern of data and (b) use this function to predict values of one factor, given known values of any number of factors in a data set. (3)

Representative Sample: A sample in which the characteristics of individuals, items, or data in the sample resemble those in a population of interest. (12)

Sample: A set of selected individuals, items, or data taken from a population of interest. (12)

Sampling Bias: A type of bias when a sampling procedure employed favors certain data types or groups over others, resulting in a nonrepresentative sample. (12)

Sampling Error: The extent to which sample statistics selected from the same population differ from one another. (12)

Sampling With Replacement: A sampling procedure in which each selection is replaced before the next selection is made. (12)

Sampling Without Replacement: A sampling procedure in which each selection is not replaced before the next selection is made. (12)

Semantic Analysis: One of the processes for converting unstructured text data into structured data by relating syntactic structures, including phrases, sentences, and paragraphs to the overall writing to derive language-independent meanings. (7)

SEMMA: An analytics program that employs five phases: Sample, Explore, Modify, Model, and Assess. (3)

Sentiment Analysis: Automated process for computationally locating, ordering, and summarizing opinions found in text, particularly with the goal of determining whether the writer has a positive, neutral, or negative view of a specific product, service, or topic. (9)

Signal: Data or information of interest from which actionable decisions can be made. (13)

Significance: A decision made concerning a value stated in the null hypothesis. When the null hypothesis is rejected, we decide that an effect exists. When the null hypothesis is retained, we decide that an effect does not exist. (13)

Simple Random Sampling: A method of sampling data such that all individuals have an equal chance of being selected. (3, 12)

Simulation: A method for implementing an existing model, statistically or over time, to test how the system that it represents will perform. (3)

Six Sigma: An analytics methodology used to improve business processes by utilizing data-based decision analytics models. (3)

Specialty Pharmacy: A pharmacy that focuses on dispensing, case management, therapy compliance, and other services for patients with complex diseases requiring high-cost medicine and high-touch care. (8)

Statistical Power: The likelihood that a sample can detect an effect in a population, assuming the effect actually exists. (12)

Stratified Random Sampling: A method of sampling in which a population is divided into subgroups or strata; data are then selected from each subgroup using simple random sampling and are combined into one overall sample. (3, 12)

Structured Data: Data that are characterized as being clearly formatted, linear, objective, quantitative, and repeatable. (9)

Structured Query Language (SQL): A standard computer language for managing and manipulating data used to query, insert, update, and modify data. (3)

Subrogation: Substitution of one organization or person by another with regard to an insurance claim, resulting in the transfer of any associated duties and rights. (10)

Systematic Sampling: A method of sampling in which the first individual is selected using simple random sampling, then every *n*th person is systematically selected until all participants have been selected. (3, 12)

Test Set: A subset of a larger data set used to test an analytics model to assess the strength and utility of a predictive relationship. (3)

Third Party Administrator: An entity that intakes and processes insurance claims or certain aspects of benefit plans for a client organization. (10)

Training Set: A subset of a larger data set used to build or train a valid analytics model to discover potentially predictive relationships. (3)

Triggers: Decision points, or inflection points, where data indicate the need for decisions to be made. (13)

Undersampling: A sampling strategy that adjusts down certain types of individuals or data, particularly for characteristics that are less represented in a population. (12)

Unstructured Data: Data that are characterized as being intuitive, language based, qualitative, and subjective. (9)

Value: The importance, usefulness, or worth generated by deliverables in a given system. (1)

Value Management: A strategic approach to advance and sustain an appropriate alignment between the results desired by customers and stakeholders and the resources needed to achieve optimal results. (4)

Index

About the Authors

James J. Gillespie, PhD, JD, MPA, is an Assistant Professor and Director of the Academy for Creativity and Leadership in the Department of Health Management and Informatics at the University of Central Florida, where he teaches health-care finance and health-care informatics. He was Founder and Coleader of the Working Group on Innovation & Interoperability, a health-care analytics project featuring leading executives from Blue Cross Blue Shield Association, Deloitte, Healthcare Information and Management Systems Society, Metropolitan Chicago Healthcare Council, Philips Healthcare, and Walgreens. His research has appeared in *Academy of Management Review, American Behavioral Scientist, European Journal of Social Psychology, Federal Reserve Bank, Harvard Business Review, Human Resource Development Review,* and *Strategic Management Journal.* His current health-care scholarship focuses on (i) analytics/informatics, (ii) economics/finance, and (iii) innovation/transformation. Dr. Gillespie previously taught at Illinois Institute of Technology, Northwestern University, University of Illinois System, University of Maryland System, and University of Wisconsin System. His education includes Northwestern University Kellogg School of Management, MA, PhD; Harvard University School of Law, JD; Princeton University Woodrow Wilson School of Public Policy, MPA; Massachusetts Institute of Technology, BS; and Carnegie Mellon University.

Gregory J. Privitera, PhD, is a Professor and Chair of the Department of Psychology at St. Bonaventure University where he is a recipient of their highest teaching honor, *The Award for Professional Excellence in Teaching*, and their highest honor for scholarship, *The Award for Professional Excellence in Research and Publication.* He also periodically teaches analytics courses in the School of Business. Dr. Privitera received his PhD in

Behavioral Neuroscience at the State University of New York at Buffalo, and completed postdoctoral work at Arizona State University. He has authored over a dozen books on topics related to statistics, methodology, and health. He has further published dozens of peer-reviewed papers on topics related to the global sociopsychological, policy, and clinical impact of obesity and mental health on strategically managing efficiencies for diagnosis, treatment, and cost, largely in health-care settings. He is an award-winning textbook author, and his research was recognized nationally by the American Psychological Association in 2015. Dr. Privitera is a veteran of the U.S. Marine Corps, an identical twin, and married with two children: a daughter, Grace, and a son, Aiden.

About the Contributors

Laurie Branch, MBA, MA, PhD, serves as President and CEO of the Iroquois Group, Inc. which helps over 2,000 insurance agencies in the United States offer policies to their customers. She was named one of the "Hot 100" industry power players and honored as among the "Elite Women in Insurance" by *Insurance Business America* magazine. She also received the New York State Women of Excellence Award for Business from Governor David Patterson in 2009. She is a professor at St. Bonaventure University's School of Business.

Puneet S. Chahal, DPM, FACFAS, FAPWH is a practicing Podiatric Surgeon at Olean Podiatry, PC. He has been in practice for 15 years. Dr. Chahal is board certified by the American Board of Foot and Ankle Surgery and Academy of Physicians in Wound Healing. He is on staff at Olean General Hospital, where he is currently serving as the Chief of Surgery and has been honored as a Golden Stethoscope Award Recipient. Dr. Chahal and his wife, Colleen, enjoy being involved in their local community and traveling with their four children.

Patrick C. Cunningham, MFA, is an account executive at Datica where he works with health systems and enterprise digital health vendors on secure, scalable, and compliant cloud computation strategies and execution. His work has included projects ranging from helping a prestigious academic medical center informatics division start their migration to a cloud-based health system to helping one of the most-used digital health vendors in the United States plan and begin execution of a nationwide interoperability initiative. He also serves as Senior Adviser to the Chicago Life Science Consortium. He attributes his perennial passion for health-care improvement to an early research fellowship with the Rehabilitation Institute of Chicago on human machine interface for stroke champions and others with cognitive disabilities.

Star* Cunningham, MBA, is Founder and CEO of 4D Healthware, LLC. She has extensive global business executive experience that has taken her to every continent, with the exception of Antarctica, in addition to living in South Africa, Vietnam, and New Zealand. She is a successful serial entrepreneur and recognized expert on "smart" (M2M learning) systems and wearable technology. Star is frequently asked by public and private companies and the media to contribute her expertise regarding innovative health management solutions, patient engagement tools and quantifiable health measures. Her expertise also includes big data, leadership, strategic planning, and technology.

Matthew Dreckmeier, PharmD, is a clinical pharmacist at OptumHealth. He is a highly respected professional pharmacist and health-care executive, with deep experience in multiple components of the pharmacy sector. His expertise includes clinical research, community pharmacy, geriatrics, medication therapy management, pharmacogenomics/pharmacogenetics, and pharmacy automation. He is currently a clinical pharmacist at OptumHealth, part of UnitedHealth Group, a diversified health and well-being company dedicated to helping people live healthier lives and making the health system work better for everyone. Matt's prior experience includes pharmacist roles at Meijer, Walgreens, and Medco. He holds a Doctor of Pharmacy (PharmD) from Ohio Northern University.

Joseph P. Gaspero is the CEO and Cofounder of Center for Healthcare Innovation, a non-profit interdisciplinary research and education institute aimed at stimulating health-care innovation. He is a health-care executive, strategist, researcher, and thought leader. Joseph conducts research initiatives focusing on patient-driven health care, patient engagement, clinical trials, drug pricing, diversity in the health sector and other pressing health-care issues. He also leads educational workshops and symposia around the country that bring together other health-care innovators to discuss crucial issues impacting health care.

Sherri Matis-Mitchell, PhD, is an independent senior consultant for text and data analytics at Data Star Insights, serving the life sciences industries. She is a senior informatics professional with experience in natural language processing (NLP) and informatics, including data leadership roles at AstraZeneca and Elsevier. She has a wide breadth of expertise in knowledge engineering, data science, natural language processing, genomics and biomedical informatics. Sherri received her PhD in Molecular Biology from the University of Pittsburgh School of Medicine and did her postdoctoral work in Informatics at Oak Ridge National Laboratory where she contributed to the Human Genome Project.

Gail Speedy Mayeaux is Executive Director of Universal Primary Care (UPC), a federally qualified health center serving rural Cattaraugus and Allegany counties in New York State. She was the architect of a turnaround strategy that transformed a struggling, near-bankrupt clinic into a Section 330 federal grantee with an annual award exceeding $2.2 million. UPC serves just under 10,000 patients across two counties by delivering care through four clinic sites.

Edwin K. Morris, MS, CKMP, is the President and Founder of Pioneer Knowledge Services (PKS), the first knowledge management nonprofit in the United States. PKS's mission is to inspire cultures that value knowledge. He joined the part-time faculty at Kent State University's Information Architecture and Knowledge Management graduate program in Spring 2015. In the fall of 2016, he began a secondary appointment for another Kent State entity at the School of Digital Sciences.

Platen Petrov, PhD, is the Director of Cognitive Technology at KPMG and was previously a partner with IBM Watson AI and Data Platform cognitive practice. He is an adjunct professor at University of Illinois at Chicago where he teaches Natural Language Processing and Cognitive Analytics. Dr. Petrov is an authority on implementing transformational business solutions enabled through artificial intelligence (AI) and advanced analytics. Dr. Petrov earlier served as executive director and Chief Enterprise Architect for Blue Cross Blue Shield Association overseeing a large portfolio of transactional and analytical systems.

Steven Press, MSPM, PMP, is an Operations Research Analyst with the Department of Homeland Security. In 2016, he received the Buffalo Federal Executive Board's Exceptional Service Award for his leadership implementing a data analytics solution within the US Citizenship and Immigration Services (USCIS). He has 15 years of experience in the fields of operations research, business analysis, and project management for companies such as Ingram Micro, Mattel, and HSBC bank. He has successfully implemented several projects related to data analytics and business intelligence.

Andrew J. Privitera, MBA, is the franchise owner of a Chick-fil-A Restaurant in Omaha, NE. He is certified as a Lean Six Sigma Black Belt and is a retired U.S. Army Soldier. His background includes 21 years of military service from which he retired honorably at the highest enlisted rank, Sergeant Major. He is a successful business owner and is actively engaged in his community where he currently serves on the boards of directors for four community nonprofit organizations.

Derek E. Walton, PMP, is a Project Manager of large-scale nuclear engineering projects for Duke Energy and an MBA student at the University of North Carolina at Wilmington. In his previous role, he served as a Financial Analyst for Duke Energy to develop performance metrics for the nuclear fleet and to support financial strategies as a subject matter expert. He has additional experience as an analyst in global therapeutic studies for a contract research organization to foster insights into health-care analytics modeling.

Daniel Yunker, MBA, is President of Clear Spring Health. He is an innovative health-care executive with an extensive background of leading health-care organizations and a keen eye for identifying and executing upon process improvement, collaboration, and profitable growth opportunities. With his proven skill set in all phases of strategic, financial, and organizational culture, as well as hands-on attributes of executive leadership, Dan is a respected leader of cross-functional teams. He is known for developing sound and creative business strategies that increase reimbursement, innovate, and advance efforts for transformation that deliver sustainable financial, human capital, operational and clinical performance. This includes a demonstrated ability for building programs from the ground up, as well as enhancing, reengineering and leveraging existing operations.

www.ingramcontent.com/pod-product-compliance
Ingram Content Group UK Ltd.
Pitfield, Milton Keynes, MK11 3LW, UK
UKHW020210290926
15470UKWH00001B/114

9 781498 550970